DIVING
BERMUDA

DIVING
BERMUDA

BY JESSE CANCELMO AND MIKE STROHOFER

AQUA QUEST PUBLICATIONS, INC. ■ NEW YORK

PUBLISHER'S NOTE

The Aqua Quest *Diving* series offers extensive information on dive sites as well as topside activities.

At the time of publication, the information contained in this book was determined to be as accurate and up-to-date as possible. The reader should bear in mind, however, that dive site terrain and landmarks change due to weather or construction. In addition, new dive shops, restaurants, hotels and stores can open and existing ones close. Telephone numbers are subject to change as are government regulations.

The publisher welcomes the reader's comments and assistance to help ensure the accuracy of future editions of this book.

Good diving and enjoy your stay!

Library of Congress Cataloging-in-Publication Data

Cancelmo, Jesse.
    Diving Bermuda / by Jesse Cancelmo & Mike Strohofer—
        2nd ed.
    p.   cm.
    Includes index.
    ISBN 10: 1-881652-20-3; ISBN 13: 978-1-881652-20-5
    1. Scuba diving—Bermuda Islands—Guidebooks. 2.
    Bermuda islands—Guidebooks. I. Strohofer, Mike.
    II. Title.
GV838.673.B46C36 2003
797.2'3—dc21
                                            2003002563

Cover: Sarah Cancelmo ascends from the *Hermes*, one of Bermuda's most recent and popular shipwrecks. Photo: J. Cancelmo.

Title page: A diver watches a porgy glide beneath one of the massive paddle wheels of the steamer *Nola*, sunk in 1863. Photo: J. Cancelmo.

Second Edition
Printed in China
10 9 8 7 6 5 4 3 2 1

Design by Richard Liu.

Acknowledgements

Special thanks to Judie Clee of the Bermuda Aquarium and Dave Less of Blue Water Divers.

Dedication

To Dr. J. James Cancelmo, Jr. whose love for the sea and Bermuda will forever be inspirational.

Contents

CHAPTER VI

CHAPTER VII

CHAPTER VIII

CHAPTER IX

PREFACE

Exploring the island of Bermuda and the many reefs and shipwrecks that surround her is an exciting adventure. Since my first big find from the Spanish galleon *San Pedro* in 1955, I have located many wrecks in these treacherous waters, and each and every location is a different experience.

Treasure takes many shapes and has many values, from the cargo of the shipwreck *Caesar*, which wrecked on May 18, 1818, to the Spanish treasure wreck *San Pedro*, which sank in the fall of 1594. Although located in 1951, I was not able to commence work on the *San Pedro* until the summer of 1955, but the salvage continued for the next seven years. The prizes were worth the wait and the long years of work, for we salvaged gold, jewelry and other artifacts. The *San Pedro's* collection included a gold and emerald cross, the single most valuable treasure found in the Western Hemisphere up until that time. It was later stolen from the Bermuda Government!

This new edition of *Diving Bermuda* is highly recommended not only for the novice snorkeler, but also for the experienced diver. It offers numerous sites to explore, whether you want to fish watch or see an historic shipwreck lying in a sand hole 40 feet below.

Teddy Tucker
Hamilton, Bermuda
August 2005

FOREWORD

If you like to explore shipwrecks and coral reefs teeming with tropical fish, you'll love Bermuda. In fact, the combination of hundreds of shallow-water wrecks surrounded by colorful reefs makes this picturesque island a unique destination for scuba divers and snorkelers.

In addition, the superb beaches, excellent restaurants and exceptional shopping make Bermuda an ideal vacation spot for divers accompanied by non-diving family or friends.

This second edition of *Diving Bermuda* is a comprehensive update of the 1990 edition. In the shipwreck chapter we have added the *Lartington*, *Caesar*, *B-29* and the *Manilla* wrecks. We have also added additional reefs and snorkeling sites.

Besides a brief overview of Bermuda's past and present, we have included extensive information on the shipwrecks, reefs and marine life that surround Bermuda as well as the dive operators who can take you there. Snorkeling in Bermuda is superb, and we have devoted a special section to some of the best sites.

To augment the diving sections, we have added comprehensive information on accommodations, shopping and restaurants, as well as other aquatic activities that can be enjoyed by non-divers.

Whether you are a serious diver, holiday snorkeler, or simply an admirer of the undersea world, you will find this book a valuable reference that contains a wealth of useful information. We hope you enjoy it.

Jesse Cancelmo, Houston, Texas
Michael Strohofer, Mainesville, Ohio
August 2005

CHAPTER I   BERMUDA

A Maritime Legacy

THE PAST

Fascinating tales of seafaring and shipwrecked sailors are woven throughout Bermuda's history. The Spaniard Juan de Bermudez first discovered this remote island in 1503, but the Spanish did not settle. For decades to follow, superstitious sailors referred to Bermuda as the "Isle of Devils" because of the treacherous reefs that encircled it. Navigating the shallow reefs around Bermuda was a hazardous undertaking for the sailing ships of that era and, consequently, few landfalls were made.

In 1609, the English flagship *Sea Venture*, under command of Admiral Sir George Somers, was leading a flotilla of eight ships bound for Jamestown Colony in Virginia when she became separated from the fleet in a storm. The storm blew the *Sea Venture* against a reef off the east end of Bermuda where she was wrecked. All the crew made it to shore safely. For ten months, while they labored to build two boats, the crew lived off the island's abundant supply of turtles, pigeons, fruit, fish and the wild pigs descended from Spanish stock.

When they eventually reached Virginia, their reports of the island aroused great interest and, in 1612, King James extended the Charter of the Virginia Company to include Bermuda. That same year, sixty English colonists founded St. George's which is is now the oldest continuously inhabited English-speaking settlement in the Western Hemisphere. Forts were soon built, and Bermuda became a key turning point for ships returning to Europe from the New World. Ships would ride the Gulf Stream north and then head east when on the same latitude as Bermuda.

The Bermuda Company was founded in 1615 and Captain Daniel Tucker was appointed the island's first governor. The island was divided into nine parishes, and the first parliament in the Western Hemisphere convened in 1620.

Ship building, using Bermuda's native cedar, and whaling were the mainstays of the island's early economy. Many Bermudians made their fortunes through privateering in the late 1700's while others prospered by salvaging ships

Gibbs Hill Lighthouse is prominently situated above the Southampton shoreline. Photo: J. Cancelmo.

King Neptune, a figurehead from the HMS Irresistable, *can be seen at the Maritime Museum on Ireland Island. Photo: M. Strohofer.*

wrecked on the shallow offshore reefs. During this period, trade with the American colonies continued to grow.

Bermudians aided George Washington's army during the Revolutionary War. In fact, gunpowder was stolen from the government's magazine to help the American cause. During the American Civil War, Bermuda was sympathetic toward the South where it had strong trading ties. Many Confederate blockade runners were based in Bermuda and two of them—the *Mary Celestia* and the *Nola (Montana)*—remain there to this day.

In the early 20th century, agriculture formed the bulwark of the economy. During these years, the Bermuda onion became known throughout the world for its sweetness.

Tourism became increasingly significant in the 1930's and by the 1950's, rose to be the leading factor in the island's economy. Today, tourism accounts for more than 70 percent of the island's income, and Bermuda is visited by more than 500,000 vacationers each year. It ranks as one of the most-returned-to vacation spots in the world. More than 90 percent of these tourists are Americans.

During both World Wars, Bermuda hosted important military bases. In 1941, as part of the lend-lease agreement for American destroyers, Britain gave the United States a 99-year lease on naval and air bases. The Naval Air Station was closed in 1993.

In 1968, a new constitution granted internal self-government to Bermuda. The British Crown-appointed governor maintains responsibility for external affairs, defense, internal security and the police, but acts on advice of the government leaders.

The Present

Bermuda is a subtropical archipelago located about 650 miles (1048 km) southeast of Cape Hatteras, North Carolina. The island is on the same latitude as Savannah and Dallas and due north of San Juan, Puerto Rico.

Although Bermuda is actually a fishhook-shaped string of seven main islands interconnected by a series of bridges, it is considered to be one geographic unit and referred to as the Island of Bermuda. There are also more than 150 smaller islands within the main islands, most of them uninhabited. Bermuda proper is 21 miles (34 km) long and less than 2 miles (3.2 km) wide at its center. It is a hilly island, lush in vegetation with miles of pink sand beaches, limestone cliffs, and dramatic scenery. Its highest elevation is 260 feet (79 m) above sea level.

Almost 63,000 people, including about 7,000 Americans, live on its 21 square miles (54 sq km), yet Bermuda's most valuable resource—its environment—has been protected wisely. The main industry continues to be tourism, and there are more than a hundred hotels, guest houses and cottage colonies on the island. Yet, there are no billboards, bright lights, neon signs, high-rises, parking meters, or fast food strips. And, the speed limit is still 20 miles (32 km) an hour!

Bermuda is a self governing British Dependent Territory. Illiteracy and unemployment are almost nonexistent, and Bermuda has no income tax or national debt. According to World Bank figures, Bermuda's residents enjoy one of the highest per capita incomes in the world. Bermudians are proud of their island, and treat visitors with warm and friendly hospitality.

Bermuda's south shore beaches like this one at Warwick Long Bay, are known for excellent snorkeling. Photo: J. Cancelmo.

Brightly colored local fishing boats
can be seen in Bermuda's many
coves and mooring areas. Photo:
J. Cancelmo.

Cruise ship passengers can also
take advantage of Bermuda's
beautiful sunsets. Photo:
M. Strohofer.

USEFUL INFORMATION

Climate. Bermuda's climate ranges from subtropical to temperate. Although situated well to the north of the Caribbean, there are coconut palms, citrus fruits and warm, Caribbean-like waters.

Bermuda is insulated by the Gulf Stream to the west and north which minimizes weather extremes. Frosts and freezes are unheard of. There are two seasons in Bermuda, a long summer and a short winter. It rarely gets above 90 degrees F (32 degrees C) in the summer with a daytime average of 80 F (27 C). Winter averages 71 degrees F (22 C) and hardly ever drops below 60 F (16 C). There is no rainy or dry season and the 60 inches (1500 mm) of annual rainfall are evenly spread throughout the year. There has never been a year with less than 340 days of sunshine. From December to April, it is usually windy.

Vegetation thrives in Bermuda, and flowers heavily scent the air. Many parts of the narrow, winding roads are lined with red, pink and white oleanders, southern hibiscus and bougainvillea.

Getting There. Bermuda is a mere 1 hour and 50 minutes by air from New York. Non-stop flights are also available from London, Toronto, Atlanta, Baltimore, Boston, Charlotte, St. Louis and Philadelphia. Cruise ships from New York, Boston, Philadelphia, Charleston and Ft. Lauderdale call on Bermuda.

Entry and Exit Requirements. A return ticket as well as a passport, voter's registration card or birth certificate with a photo ID are required for entry. With recent tightening of security a passport may soon be required for re-entry into the U.S. A $20 tax is collected on departure. Check with U.S. Customs for the latest information on duty free allowances (currently $600 per person) on return to the U.S.

The beacon from St. David's Lighthouse can be seen by mariners for 15 miles (24 km). Photo: M. Strohofer.

Island Transportation. Getting around this picturesque 21-mile (34 km) long island is uncomplicated and enjoyable. Although there are no rental cars on the island, motorbikes are available at all major hotels. Other means of transportation include taxis, the pink-and-blue Bermuda buses and a very convenient ferry system. Driving is on the left side and the speed limit is a leisurely 20 miles an hour (32 kph), except in Hamilton where the limit is 10 miles an hour (16 kph). The obvious courtesy given to pedestrians by Bermudian motorists is a pleasant surprise for American visitors. Tours by taxi, horse-drawn carriage and boat are readily available.

Dress. Daytime wear in Bermuda is informal but not as casual as some tourists would like. It is considered unacceptable for men to be shirtless or barefoot except at the beach. For women, bare feet, short-shorts and bathing suits are strictly beachwear.

Bermuda shorts are considered both formal and informal attire and are worn by the island's businessmen, government officials and the police, or "bobbies," as they are called. At most hotels, men are requested to wear jackets and ties for dinner after 6 P.M. Women are expected to wear dresses. There are, however, several dining spots to choose from where casual clothes are acceptable. The evenings are cool, so sweaters are advisable.

Even in the middle of summer, rainshowers generally last for only an hour, but are common, so a raincoat is suggested if you plan to do a lot of walking or motorbiking.

Rented motorbikes are an easy and fun way to get around the island.
Photo: J. Cancelmo.

THE CITY OF HAMILTON

The City of Hamilton, founded in 1790, is located in Pembroke Parish in the middle of the island. Hamilton is Bermuda's main commercial and business center, and has been the island's capital since 1815 when the legislature was moved from St. George's. Hosting a quarter of the island's population, Hamilton is a busy city complete with rush hour traffic. Bustling Front Street runs along the harbor's edge with a row of fine stores on one side and usually a line-up of luxury cruise ships on the other side. In the middle of Front Street, at the intersection with Queen Street, is the famous and colorful "birdcage" where Bermuda bobbies theatrically direct the busy traffic. Hamilton offers exciting shopping, excellent dining and hours of sightseeing possibilities. Sites to see include the Par-la-Ville Gardens, the historic Perot Post Office, the Bermuda Library, the Historical Society and Colonial Archives, Fort Hamilton, the Cabinet Building and Sessions House, City Hall and Art Gallery, and Victoria Park.

The City of Hamilton as seen from Hamilton Harbour. Photo: J. Cancelmo.

*Bermuda's south shore has stretches
of limestone cliffs and is riddled with
jagged outcrops and boiler reefs.
Photo: J. Cancelmo.*

Currency. The monetary unit is the Bermuda dollar (BD$), although United States currency is accepted everywhere and the two are interchangeable and identical in value.

Electricity. Electricity is 110 volts, 60 cycles, which is the standard in the United States.

Telephone. The telephone system is modern and reliable. Direct dialing service is available to the United States, Canada, United Kingdom and Australia, as well as to many islands in the Caribbean. To direct dial Bermuda from the United States, use area code 441 plus the Bermuda code, either 29 or 23, followed by the five-digit local number.

Time. Bermuda is in the Atlantic Standard Time Zone, one hour ahead of Eastern Standard Time. Daylight Savings Time is observed.

Medical. Medical services, doctors and dentists are on a private system similar to that in the United States. Fees are reasonable and the availability of general practitioners is good.

Water. The source of most drinking water is either captured rain or desalinated water. The quality is excellent. Conservation is a way of life in Bermuda.

Parishes. Bermuda is divided into nine parishes. From west to east, they are: Sandy's, Southampton,Warwick, Paget, Pembroke, Devonshire, Smith's, Hamilton, and St. George's. The town of St. George's and the City of Hamilton are considered separate corporations.

THE TOWN OF ST. GEORGE'S

St. George's is a delightful old town, packed full of Bermuda history, located on the far eastern end of the island. Named after the patron saint of England, St. George's was founded in 1612 and preceded Hamilton as Bermuda's capital. Most of the buildings, streets and alleys are reminiscent of the 1600's. King's Square, in the heart of St. George's, has cedar replicas of Stocks and Pillory. The beautifully restored Town Hall is the administrative headquarters for St. George's. Across the bridge on Ordnance Island is a replica of the *Deliverance*, one of the first ships built in Bermuda by the Jamestown colonists who survived the wreck of the *Sea Venture* in 1609. Another form of 17th century punishment, the Ducking Stool, is also located on Ordnance Island. Other points of interest include St. Peter's Church, the oldest Protestant Church in the Western Hemisphere, the Confederate Museum, Gunpowder Cavern, Somers Garden and the State House, which is the oldest (1620) house in Bermuda constructed entirely of limestone.

St. George's Harbour.
Photo: M. Strohofer.

CHAPTER II   ACCOMMODATIONS

For All Budgets

When it comes to a place to stay, Bermuda offers many options including large resort hotels, small hotels, clubs, housekeeping cottages, time-sharing apartments and guest houses. Another type of accommodation that is uniquely Bermudian is the cottage colony. These are small communities of cottages that usually have a pool, a private beach, tennis courts, a clubhouse and a dining room. In addition, kitchenettes are often available. Most are surrounded by lush property, meticulously landscaped. Guests can enjoy their privacy and have the opportunity to socialize if they wish.

There is usually a service charge of about 10 percent and a 6 percent hotel tax which, in most cases, is automatically added to the bill. Be sure to inquire when you are quoted a room price. Off-season prices are generally 25 percent less.

Large Hotels. More than 100 rooms. $150 to $250 a day per person based on double occupancy.

Small Hotels. Under 100 rooms. $100 to $200+ a day per person based on double occupancy.

Cottages and Efficiency Apartments. 25-100 rooms. Most have kitchenettes. $50 to $100 a day per person based on double occupancy.

Guest Houses. Under 25 rooms. $40 to $75 a day per person based on double occupancy. No sports facilities, meals or restaurants.

Reef's Beach provides an ideal setting for a day of relaxation in the sun. Photo: J. Cancelmo.

A number of hotels offer their guests beautiful private beaches. Photo: J. Cancelmo.

	Modified American Plan (Breakfast & Dinner Included)	Bermuda Plan (Breakfast Included)	Continental Plan (Continental Breakfast Included)	European Plan (No Meals Included)	Credit Card Accepted	Swimming Pool	Tennis Courts	Private Beach
DEVONSHIRE PARISH Cottages/Efficiencies								
Ariel Sands Beach Club 800-468-6610, 441-236-1010		■			■	■	■	■
Guest Houses								
Burch's Guest Apartments 800-637-4110, 441-292-5746				■		■		
HAMILTON PARISH Large Hotels								
Grotto Bay Beach Hotel 800-582-3190 US, 800-463-0851 Can, 441-293-8333	■	■		■	■	■	■	■
Guest Houses								
The Clear View Suites 800-468-9600, 441-293-0484		■	■	■	■	■	■	
PAGET PARISH Large Hotels								
Elbow Beach Hotel 800-344-3526, 441-236-3535		■		■	■	■	■	■
Small Hotels								
Harmony Club 800-427-6664, 441-236-3500	■				■	■	■	
Newstead 800-468-4111, 441-236-6060		■			■	■	■	
Stonington Beach Hotel 800-457-4060, 441-236-5416	■	■			■	■	■	■
White Sands Hotel & Cottages 800-548-0547, 441-236-2023	■	■			■	■		

	Modified American Plan (Breakfast & Dinner Included)	Bermuda Plan (Breakfast Included)	Continental Plan (Continental Breakfast Included)	European Plan (No Meals Included)	Credit Card Accepted	Swimming Pool	Tennis Courts	Private Beach
Cottages/Efficiencies								
Fourways Inn 800-962-7654, 441-236-6517	■		■		■	■		
Horizons & Cottages 800-468-0022, 441-236-0048	■	■			■	■	■	
Guest Houses								
Barnsdale Guest Apartments 441-236-0164				■	■	■		
Dawkins Manor 441-236-7419				■		■		
Grape Bay Cottages 800-637-4116, 441-295-7017				■	■			■
Greenbank and Cottages 800-637-4116 US, 800-267-7600 Can, 441-236-3615			■	■	■			
Little Pomander 441-236-7635			■		■			
Loughlands 441-236-1253			■			■	■	
Paraquet Guest Apartments 441-236-5842				■	■			
Salt Kettle House 441-236-0407		■						
Sky Top Cottages 887-689-4043, 441-236-7984				■	■			
Valley Cottages and Apartments 800-637-4116, 441-236-0628				■	■			
PEMBROKE PARISH **Large Hotels**								
The Princess 800-203-3222, 441-295-5608				■	■	■	■	

	MODIFIED AMERICAN PLAN Breakfast & Dinner Included	BERMUDA PLAN Breakfast Included	CONTINENTAL PLAN Continental Breakfast Included	EUROPEAN PLAN No Meals Included	CREDIT CARD ACCEPTED	SWIMMING POOL	TENNIS COURTS	PRIVATE BEACH
Small Hotels								
Hamilton Hotel and Island Club 800-203-3222, 441-295-5608				■	■	■	■	
Rosedon 800-742-5008, 441-295-1640		■			■	■		
Royal Palms Hotel 800-678-0783 US, 800-799-0824 Can, 441-292-1854			■		■	■		
Waterloo House 800-468-4100, 809-295-4480	■	■		■	■	■		
Cottages/Efficiencies								
La Casa Del Masa 441-292-8726				■	■	■		
Marula Guest Apartments 441-295-2893				■	■	■		
Rosemont 800-367-0040, 441-292-1055				■	■	■		
Guest Houses								
Edgehill Manor 441-295-7124			■			■		
Fordham Hall Guest House 441-295-1551			■		■			
Hi-Roy 441-292-0808	■	■						
Marzarine-By-The-Sea 441-292-1690				■	■	■		
Oxford House 800-548-7758, 441-295-0503			■		■			
Robin's Nest 800-637-4116, 441-292-4347				■		■		

	MODIFIED AMERICAN PLAN Breakfast & Dinner Included	BERMUDA PLAN Breakfast Included	CONTINENTAL PLAN Continental Breakfast Included	EUROPEAN PLAN No Meals Included	CREDIT CARD ACCEPTED	SWIMMING POOL	TENNIS COURTS	PRIVATE BEACH
SANDY'S PARISH **Small Hotels**								
Willowbank 800-752-8493 US, 800-463-8444 Can, 441-234-1616	■				■	■	■	■
Cottages/Efficiencies								
Cambridge Beaches 800-468-7300 US, 800-463-5990 Can, 441-234-0331	■				■	■	■	■
Daniel's Head Village 800-225-4255		■			■		■	■
Lantana 800-468-3733, 441-234-0141	■				■	■	■	■
Garden House 441-234-1435				■		■		
SMITH'S PARISH **Small Hotels**								
Palmetto Suites 800-982-0026, 441-293-2323	■	■			■	■		■
Cottages/Efficiences								
Angel's Grotto 441-293-1986				■	■			
Pink Beach Club and Cottages 800-355-6161, 441-293-1666	■	■			■	■	■	■
Guest Houses								
Brightside Apartments 441-292-8410				■	■			

	Modified American Plan (Breakfast & Dinner Included)	Bermuda Plan (Breakfast Included)	Continental Plan (Continental Breakfast Included)	European Plan (No Meals Included)	Credit Card Accepted	Swimming Pool	Tennis Courts	Private Beach
ST. GEORGE'S PARISH Cottages/Efficiencies								
The St. George's Club 441-297-1200				■	■	■	■	
Small Hotels								
Aunt Nea's Inn 441-297-1630			■		■	■		
SOUTHAMPTON PARISH Large Hotels								
Wyndham Resort and Spa 800-766-3782, 441-238-8122				■	■	■	■	■
Fairmont Southampton Princess 800-441-1414				■	■	■	■	■
Small Hotels								
Pompano Beach Club 800-343-4155, 441-234-0222	■	■			■	■	■	■
The Reefs 800-742-2008, 441-238-0222	■	■			■	■	■	■
Cottages/Efficiencies								
Munro Beach Cottages 800-637-4116, 441-234-1175				■	■			■
Ocean Terrace 800-637-4116, 441-238-0019				■	■	■		
Sound View Cottage 441-238-0064				■		■		
Guest Houses								
Green's Guest House 441-238-0834, 441-238-2532		■				■		

	Modified American Plan (Breakfast & Dinner Included)	Bermuda Plan (Breakfast Included)	Continental Plan (Continental Breakfast Included)	European Plan (No Meals Included)	Credit Card Accepted	Swimming Pool	Tennis Courts	Private Beach
Royal Heights Guest House 441-238-0043			■		■	■		
WARWICK PARISH **Small Hotels**								
Breakers Beach Club and Hotel 441-236-5031				■	■	■		■
Surf Side Beach Club 800-553-9990, 441-236-7100	■	■	■	■	■	■		■
Cottages/Efficiencies								
Astwood Cove 800-637-4116 US, 800-563-9799 Can, 441-236-0984				■	■	■		
Blue Horizons 441-236-6350				■	■	■		
Clairfont Apartments 441-238-0149				■	■	■		
Granaway Guest House 441-236-3747			■		■	■		
Marley Beach Cottages 800-637-4116, 441-236-1143				■	■	■		■
Sandpiper Apartments 800-637-4116, 441-236-7093				■	■	■		
South View Guest Apartments 800-441-7087, 441-236-5257				■	■			
Syl-Den Apartments 800-637-4116, 441-238-1834				■	■	■		
Vienna Guest Apartments 800-637-4116 US, 800-267-7600 Can, 441-236-3300				■	■	■		

CHAPTER **III** SHOPPING

A British Flair

Shopping in Bermuda has a distinctly British flair. The best bargains are china, crystal and woolen goods imported from the United Kingdom. Perfume is also less expensive in Bermuda than in the United States and Canada. These items can be found in the main department stores such as **A.S. Cooper Company**, **H.A. & E. Smith, Ltd.** and **Trimingham's**. These stores have branches in both the City of Hamilton and the Town of St. George's. All major credit cards are accepted.

If you are on the lookout for a gift that is characteristically Bermudian, you might want to consider some of the Bermuda-made items that are becoming popular, such as: Gosling's Black Seal Rum, Bermuda Gold (a liqueur made from the yellow fruit of the loquat tree), Outerbridge's Sherry Peppers and sauces, Royall Lyme toilet soaps and lotions, perfume from the **Bermuda Perfumery**, or a handicraft item from the **Island Pottery.**

A policeman, or "bobbie" as they are called in Bermuda, directs traffic from the birdcage on Front Street in Hamilton. Photo: J. Cancelmo.

Picturesque Hamilton Harbour provides a placid home for local pleasure boats. Photo: J. Cancelmo.

Shoppers in downtown Hamilton
will find many bargains on
imported British goods. Photo:
J. Cancelmo.

A pleasant afternoon can be spent
browsing and shopping among
Front Street's fine shops in
downtown Hamilton. Photo:
J. Cancelmo.

SOME PROMINENT MERCHANTS

Archie Brown
Front Street in Hamilton and York Street in St. George's.
Sweaters, jackets and other woolen goods

A.S. Coopers & Sons, Ltd.
Front Street in Hamilton and York Street in St. George's.
Fine bone china, earthenware and jewelry

Astwood Dickson
Front and Queen Streets in Hamilton, the Walker Arcade in Hamilton, and most major hotels.
Jewelry and timepieces featuring products by Patek Philippe, Concord, Omega and Heuer

Bermuda Perfumery
Front and Reid Streets in Hamilton, and St. George's Square in St. George's.
Locally made perfumes and body lotions

Bluck's
Front and Par La Ville Streets in Hamilton, Water Street in St. George's and in the Southampton Princess Hotel.
China, crystal and antiques

Constables of Bermuda
York Street in St. George's.
Icelandic woolen goods from the Hilda line, including jackets, sweaters, gloves and scarves

Crisson Jewelers
Front, Reid and Queen Streets in Hamilton, and York Street in St. George's, and some major hotels.
Jewelry and timepieces including Rolex, Cartier, Longine, Ebel and Piaget

English Sports Shop
Front Street in Hamilton, Somer's Wharf in St. George's, Southampton Princess Hotel.
Sweaters, jackets and other woolen goods

H.A. & E. Smith, Ltd.
Front Street in Hamilton and York Street in St. George's.
Cashmere, Shetland and lamb's wool sweaters; British cosmetics and Liberty fabrics

The Irish Linen Shop
Front and Queen Streets in Hamilton.
Linens and fabrics, featuring dresses, shawls and bedspreads by Souleiado

Peniston-Brown Co.
Front Street in Hamilton opposite the Ferry Terminal and King's Square in St. George's.
Perfumes, including Christian Dior, Chanel, Oscar de la Renta and Nina Ricci

Scottish Wool Shop
Queen Street in Hamilton.
Woolen and cotton goods from Great Britain. Shetland, cashmere and lambswool sweaters

Trimingham's
Front Street in Hamilton and York Street in St. George's.
Cosmetics and perfumes, fine jewelry, crystal and china

Vera P. Card
Front Street West in Hamilton, and York Street in St. George's and most major hotels.
Collectibles featuring Lladró and Hummel figurines, and products by Rosenthal, Goebel and Swarovski

CHAPTER **IV** DINING

Chips to Gourmet Fare

The Bermuda telephone directory lists more than 150 restaurants, which means there are more than seven per square mile.

Bermudian restaurants offer a wide selection of menus ranging from chicken and hamburgers at the **Specialty Inn** to lobster newberg at the **Newport Room** in the Southampton Princess Hotel. British fare, such as fish and chips, Yorkshire pudding, and steak and kidney pie, is available at a number of restaurants including the **Colony Pub**, the **Swizzle Inn**, and the **Hog Penny**.

Bermudian dishes include fresh local fish preparations, mussel pie, black rum cake and cassava pie. One specialty of note is fish chowder laced with black rum and sherry peppers.

Sunday brunch is a time-honored tradition in Bermuda and should not be missed. Codfish and potatoes served with fresh vegetables and cooked bananas is a favorite, though salty dish. The major hotels offer Sunday brunches with presentations elaborate enough to turn a king's head.

Jackets and ties are required at most of the expensive and moderately priced restaurants.

In all but the fast food reataurants, a 15 percent service charge is normally added to the bill. Although most restaurants accept major credit cards, it is a good idea to inquire when making reservations.

Bermuda's rock formations mesh nicely with sea and sand creating an idyllic setting for a peaceful walk on the beach. Photo: J. Cancelmo.

Dining with a sunset view from one of Bermuda's many excellent restaurants is a fitting way to cap the day's activities. Photo: J. Cancelmo.

EXPENSIVE

Café Lido At Elbow Beach   236-9884

For an elegant dining experience literally on the beach, try this local favorite at the Elbow Beach Hotel. Don't let the name fool you, there is nothing café-ish about this romantic dining spot; it is a full-service, upscale event. Popular with the locals for special occasions, there is usually a crowd, but the no-reservation policy adopted by many American restaurants hasn't made its way to Bermuda yet. The Saturday night buffet is a seafood extravaganza not to be missed if you love fare such as mussels, shrimp and lobster.

Fourways Inn   236-6516

This gourmet restaurant, housed in an impressive eighteenth century Georgian structure, is located on Middle Road in Paget. The fresh local fish sauteed in tomato, fish and cream sauce is highly recommended. Dinner is served from 7:00 until 9:30, with brunches on Thursday and Sunday. Lunch is served only from April through October.

Henry VIII Pub & Restaurant   238-1977
238-0908

This establishment features a more relaxed atmosphere than most other top restaurants. It is located just below Gibb's Hill Lighthouse, across from the Wyndham Beach Resort and Spa in Southampton. The menu is well-rounded, with an excellent selection of soups and salads. There is nightly entertainment in the attached Pub with preferential seating for restaurant patrons. Dinner is served from 7:00 until 10:30, lunch from noon until 2:30, with sandwiches available until 4:00. Brunch is served on Sundays.

Newport Room   238-2555

One of the most exquisite restaurants on the island is in the Southampton Princess Hotel, just east of Gibb's Hill Lighthouse. The menu includes some luscious local specialties. The seafood lover should try the scallops sauteed in broth with thyme flower and olive oil. For the more robust palate, sample the filet of venison with red cabbage and cranberries. Dinner is served from 7:00 until midnight.

Tom Moore's Tavern   293-8020

Recently reopened, this tavern on Walsingham Lane was originally founded in 1652, making it the oldest restaurant on the island. The food is excellent, with local fish the specialty.

Waterlot Inn   238-8000

Don't miss the Sunday brunch at this historic inn located on the water in Southampton Parish. Its culinary repertoire ranks as one of the island's finest.

MODERATE

Carriage House   297-1730

Overlooking St. George's Harbour from Water Street, this restaurant features a basic continental cuisine. Also of note is the Sunday brunch.

Fisherman's Reef   292-1609

Located above the Hog Penny on Burnaby Street, this restaurant, as the name implies, specializes in fish diets. However, a full a la carte menu with beef and veal selections is also available.

Frog & Onion Pub   234-2900

Traditional British pub fare, along with daily seafood specials, can be found at the west end of the island at this tavern located in the historic Cooperage building at The Royal Naval Dockyard. The name comes from the nationality of the two proprietors—Carole West (The Onion) and Jean-Paul (The Frog). Visitors will find a menu laden with items such as fish & chips, bangers & mash, and toads-in-the-hole. The British beers on tap are excellent, if you don't mind them served less than ice cold. The décor is definitely geared to the nautical minded, which divers appreciate.

Wharf Tavern   297-1515

Local fish dishes are the specialty of this tavern which overlooks St. George's Harbour from Water Street. Open for lunch and dinner.

The jolthead porgy has sharp front teeth that are used to feed on sea urchins and crabs. These silver fish measure over two feet long and are easily approached. Photo: J. Cancelmo.

Numerous excellent restaurants are in view of Gibb's Hill Lighthouse. Photo: J. Cancelmo.

Spiny lobsters hide in holes and crevices during the day and come out to feed at night. Their long antennae can sometimes be spotted protruding from under a ledge, giving away their hiding place. Photo: J. Cancelmo.

Little Venice   295-3503

One of the best Italian restaurants on the island is found on Bermudiana Road. It is very popular with local residents and is always crowded. Even with reservations, one should be prepared to wait for a table. For dinner guests, there is free admission to the upstairs disco.

The Hog Penny   292-2534

This English style pub on Burnaby Street is popular with local residents for its fish and chips, draft beer and nightly entertainment. On Sundays only dinner is served.

The Lobster Pot   292-6898

Located at the corner of Bermudiana and Gorham Roads, this restaurant is known for its seafood. As one might expect, lobster is the specialty. Patrons are served Bermuda lobster during the season and Maine lobster in the off-season.

The Pickled Onion   295-2263

Located on Front Street in the heart of Hamilton, this pub-style restaurant (formerly Ye Olde Cock and Feather) boasts a popular happy hour from 4 to 7 P.M., and live music on weekends. The food is mainstream, with the seafood served either fried or grilled. Full dinners or sandwiches are available.

Rosa's Cantina   295-1920

Located on the east end of Front Street in downtown Hamilton, Rosa's represents the best Mexican food on the island. For those not particularly fond of the spicy Mexican dishes, but are tagging along because they got outvoted, Rosa's also serves mild chicken and seafood dishes.

Swizzle Inn   293-1854

Arguably the most popular watering hole on the island, it is the first bar after you leave the airport, and the last one you pass when heading back to the airport. Famous for its orange-colored swizzle and wall-to-wall business cards (Yeah, go ahead and tack yours up.), the Swizzle Inn also features live music during the season. The swizzle burger has a flavor all its own and the fish chowder is very popular. The Swizzle even has its own gift shop sporting some unique T-shirts, although they had to discontinue their old logo of "Swizzle Inn, Stagger Out" due to local pressure.

INEXPENSIVE

The Black Horse Tavern   297-1991

Far off the beaten path in St. David's is this local haunt noted for its fresh fish and generous portions. Open for lunch and dinner with carry-out service available.

Spotting a nudibranch requires a sharp eye. Photo: M. Strohofer.

Four Star Pizza 295-5555; 292-9111
232-0123; 234-2626

Hot pizzas, submarine sandwiches and chicken wings are served at four locations on the island—Hamilton, Flatts, Warwick and Somerset.

Paraquet 236-5842

Next to Elbow Beach in Paget, this casual dining establishment serves dinner daily until 1:00 A.M. On Sunday mornings, try the codfish and potatoes.

Portofino 292-2375

This popular Italian eatery, located on Bermudiana Road in Hamilton, is open for lunch Monday thru Saturday, and serves dinner daily until 1:00 A.M. On Sunday, they open at 6:00 P.M. Carry-out service is available.

Robin Hood Pub & Restaurant 295-3314

Located on Richmond Road, in the back of Hamilton, this bar and restaurant is popular with local residents on weekends. With three bars, closed circuit TV and live entertainment, the main attraction is the night life.

San Giorgio 297-1307

Located on Water Street in St. George's, this quaint little Italian restaurant only serves dinner. The owner, Nick Brown, always has an interesting daily special to go along with the standard menu items of veal, pasta and pizza. The soups and salads are excellent, but get these early since the establishment only seats fifty people.

Specialty Inn 236-3133

There are no frills and little atmosphere—just good solid food—at this inn at the bottom of Collector's Hill on South Shore Road. It is closed on Sunday.

CHAPTER V DIVING

Wrecks and Reefs

THE SEASON

The diving season is from mid-March through November, although some operations stay open year round. Most are closed from the first of the year until March. Water temperature is in the mid-80's F (27°C) from the middle of June to the end of September, and an eighth-inch (3 mm) shorty or T-shirt is sufficient. During the season's peripheral months of April and May, and October and November, a full quarter-inch (6 mm) wet suit and hood are recommended. During the coolest month, February, the water temperature can drop to the low 60's F (16°C).

Because of the cooler water temperatures, few dive during the off-season. The plus side is plenty of extra room on the dive boat, and the increased visibility due to the absence of plankton.

BERMUDA MARITIME MUSEUM

The Maritime Museum has much of interest for visiting divers. Early examples of diving gear and many shipwreck artifacts including the Teddy Tucker Treasure Collection are on display. Also of special interest is the exhibit of the Royal Navy in Bermuda, as well as the unique Brombay Bottle Collection. In addition, there is an exhibit of old Bermudian-built boats and a display of whaling paraphernalia.

The entire museum is contained within the massive ramparts of an early military fort. It is located on the far west end of the island at the Royal Navy Dockyard. Telephone 234-1418.

The combination of crystal clear water and bright sunshine provides great picture-taking possibilities for underwater photographers. Photo: J. Cancelmo.

The majestic queen angelfish flaunts a dark forehead "crown" ringed and spotted with bright blue markings. Photo: J. Cancelmo.

WRECKS AND REEFS

Imagine hundreds of shipwrecks in clear shallow water surrounded by coral reefs abundant with tropical fish and you have a good idea of what to expect in Bermuda.

More than 350 shipwrecks, dating from the 1500's to the present lie scattered around Bermuda, most victims of the treacherous fringing reef that surrounds the island. A navigator's nightmare has turned Bermuda into a wreck diver's paradise! Both the novice and experienced wreck diver will find something of interest, whether it is a Spanish galleon, a 19th century paddle steamer, or a modern freighter.

The reefs that humbled these once proud ships must not be overlooked. These are the northernmost coral reefs in the Western Hemisphere and rival those at many Caribbean dest inations.

In fact, Bermuda's fringing reef hosts a kaldeidoscopic array of coral and fish life. Most of the species found in the Caribbean can be seen here, along with a few varieties indigenous only to Bermudian waters. The colorful parrotfish and wrasse families are well respresented, as are damselfish and snappers.

Hogfish and jacks, triggerfish, tangs and trumpetfish, grunts, grasbys and grouper, porcupinefish, pompano and porgies, sandivers, sergeant majors and squirrelfish can all be seen on the reefs of Bermuda. The more retiring reef creatures such as moray eels, spiny lobsters, arrow crabs, shrimps, squid and octopus are also in abundance. Sea turtles are making a remarkable comeback and are now seen on a regular basis.

VISIBILITY

In general, the farther offshore from Bermuda the dive site is, the clearer the water. This is due to a lack of sedimentation and reduced re ef action. On the northern and western reefs, the average visibility in the summer is 100 feet (30 m). During the coldest months, it can reach 150 feet (46 m).

On the south shore and on the eastern end of the island, the reefline is much closer to shore and summer visibility is about 80 feet (24 m). Anything greater is considered a bonus. If the visibility drops below 30 feet (9 m), dive boats rarely venture out.

Tina Fisher captures a "porthole memory" on the wreck of the Hermes. Photo: J. Cancelmo.

EXPERIENCE LEVELS

Because most dive sites are shallow and well protected, novices as well as experienced divers can safely enjoy the shipwrecks and reefs. All the dive shops will provide licensed guides for novices. These guides must pass comprehensive written and open water exams.

There are no strong currents, no dangerous marine animals, and no unseaworthy dive boats. For those few spots where special caution is required, it will be noted in the description of the dive site.

TRAINING

The quality of instruction available in Bermuda is top notch. All the major certification organizations are represented, such as the Professional Association of Diving Instructors (PADI), the National Association of Underwater Instructors (NAUI), the British Sub-Aqua Club (BSAC), and Scuba Schools International (SSI).

There are several options for those interested in learning how to scuba dive.

Resort Course. The resort course is simply one lesson followed by a dive. Students are taken to a confined water location—usually a swimming pool—and given an hour-long lecture and practice session on the safe use of scuba gear. Immediately afterwards, they are transported to a reef for a shallow, guided tour. It is a good introduction to scuba if you are not able to commit the time to a certification course.

Certification Course. The certification course is a much more extensive program. Approximately 30 hours of instruction are equally divided between lecture, pool work and open water dives. The fundamentals of physics, equipment, water skills, safety and the marine environment are taught and will ultimately enable the students to dive independently of an instructor. The successful candidate receives an internationally recognized certification card—"C" card—that is good for life. This card enables the diver to enjoy scuba diving anywhere in the world.

Referral. If you don't want to spend your vacation time in the classroom or at the bottom of a swimming pool, you should consider doing the first part of your course at home and the open water dives in Bermuda.

Your instructor at home can give you a document stating that you have completed the first part of the course and refer you to another instructor from the same agency in Bermuda who will conduct the open water training.

PHOTOGRAPHY

Some dive operators offer 35mm underwater cameras for rent, and others offer inexpensive disposable-type film cameras for sale.

E-6 film processing for Ektachrome and Fujichrome slides is available on the island as are camera repairs. For print film, one hour processing is available.

Several shops now rent underwater video cameras.

EQUIPMENT

Certified divers can rent scuba gear in Bermuda, but except at Elbow Beach, shore diving is not promoted. There are no rental cars in Bermuda and the taxi drivers do not welcome wet bathing suits, let alone wet dive gear. Unless you have access to a private boat, it is suggested that dive trips be arranged through one of the island's dive shops.

Underwater photographer Phil Jones captures a close-up subject on the wreck of the Nola, a Confederate blockade runner during the American Civil War. Photo: J. Cancelmo.

A resort course in the morning can have you ocean diving in the afternoon. Photo: M. Strohofer.

The Maritime Museum at the Dockyard is a "must see" for divers interested in shipwrecks. Photo: J. Cancelmo.

Dawn breaks over St. George's Harbour. Photo: M. Strohofer.

NIGHT DIVING

Although there is only a limited amount of night diving in Bermuda, several dive shops conduct night dive trips on a demand basis during the height of the season.

If you do get a chance to night dive, you will be well rewarded. Crustaceans seem to be everywhere. The eyes of spiny lobsters, shrimps and coral crabs shine back at you from tunnels and gulleys threading through the reef. Extended polyps give hard corals a soft, fuzzy appearance. Sleeping parrotfish can be seen motionless, protected by the web-like cocoon they spin around themselves at dusk. Trumpetfish and trunkfish can be stroked if approached cautiously. Octopus and squid are often seen quickly changing color when caught in the beam of a dive light. The insomniacs of the reef are the moray eels who rarely stray far from home.

Most fish are easier to approach at night when caught in the beam of a dive light. If touched, however, they usually panic and swim off in a flash, sometimes doing harm to themselves by running into the reef. This should be kept in mind when observing or approaching fish at night.

The red night shrimp is 3 inches (7.7 cm) long and only comes out at night. Photo: J. Cancelmo.

BERMUDA

SHIPWRECKS

1. *Caraquet*
2. *Madiana*
3. *Cristobal Colon*
4. *Manilla*
5. *Taunton*
6. *Iristo*
7. *Beaumaris Castle* and *Col. William Ball*
8. *Rita Zovett*
9. *Pelinaion*
10. *Kate*
11. *Pollockshields*
12. *Minnie Breslauer*
13. *Hermes*
14. *Virginia Merchant*
15. *King*
16. *Mary Celestia*
17. *B-29 Bomber*
18. *North Carolina*
19. *Caesar*
20. *Darlington*
21. *L'Herminie*
22. *Constellation*
23. *Lartington*
24. *Nola (Montana)*

REEFS

25. South West Breaker
26. Cathedral

SNORKELING SITES

27. Tobacco Bay
28. Achilles Bay
29. John Smith's Bay
30. Shelly Bay
31. Devonshire Bay
32. Elbow Beach
33. Warwick Long Bay
    Jobson's Cove
    Stonehole Bay
    Chaplin Bay
34. Church Bay
35. Somerset Long Bay
36. Bermuda Snorkel Park

PLACES OF INTEREST

A. Bermuda Biological Station
B. Aquarium
C. Maritime Museum
D. St. David's Lighthouse
E. Gibb's Hill Lighthouse
F. Ocean Discovery Centre
G. Botanical Gardens
H. Admiralty House Park
I. Spittal Pond Nature Reserve & Spanish Rock
J. Scaur Hill Fort Park
K. Gates Fort
L. Fort St. Catherine
M. Royal Naval Dockyard

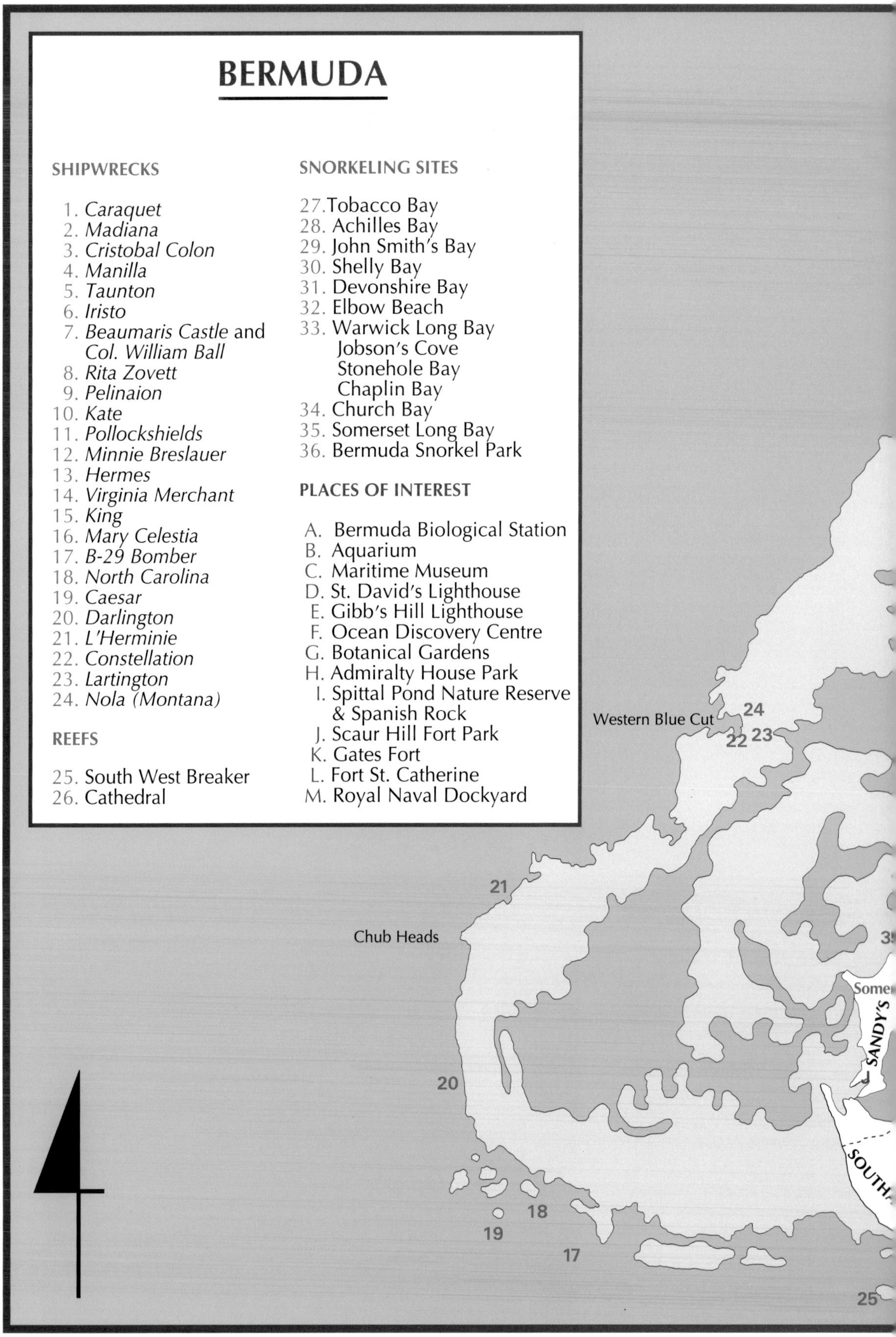

Western Blue Cut 24
22 23

21

Chub Heads

3

Some

SANDY'S

20

SOUTH

18
19
17

25

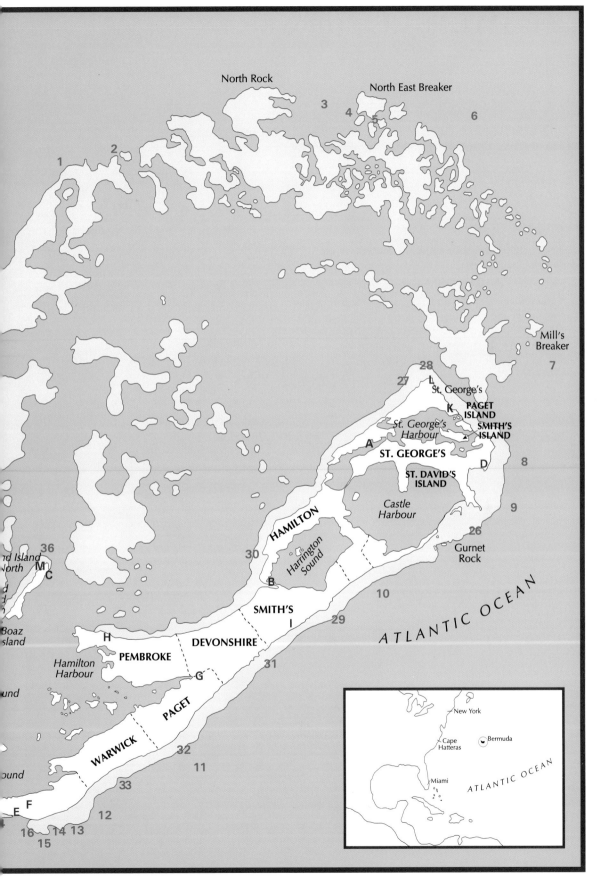

North Rock

North East Breaker

3

4

5

6

1

2

7

Mill's
Breaker

28

27

L

St. George's

PAGET
ISLAND

K

St. George's
Harbour

SMITH'S
ISLAND

A

ST. GEORGE'S

D

8

ST. DAVID'S
ISLAND

Castle
Harbour

9

26

HAMILTON

Gurnet
Rock

36

30

Harrington
Sound

nd Island
North

M

C

B

10

Boaz
sland

SMITH'S

I

29

H

DEVONSHIRE

Hamilton
Harbour

PEMBROKE

G

31

und

PAGET

WARWICK

32

11

ound

33

E

F

12

16

14

13

15

New York

Cape
Hatteras

Bermuda

Miami

ATLANTIC OCEAN

ATLANTIC OCEAN

CHAPTER **VI**   SHIPWRECKS

NORTHERN WRECKS

1. *CARAQUET*

DEPTH:	40 FEET (12 M)
SUNK:	1923
TYPE:	MAIL STEAMER
LENGTH:	ABOUT 200 FEET (61 M)

History. The *Caraquet* was a British mail steamer which also carried passengers. Her intended route was from Halifax, Nova Scotia, to Bermuda, through the West Indies, and ultimately to South America. Her last voyage ended, however, on the outer northern reefs of Bermuda.

On June 25, 1923, the master of the *Caraquet,* Captain Fernandez, was having difficulty determining his position because of rough seas and hazy conditions which made land sightings extremely difficult. He realized that he must be farther south than his calculations indicated, but he did not know how far. Under full power, his vessel ran up on the reefs three miles west of North Rock. The ship was a total loss, although all of the passengers and crew got off safely. The rough weather made removing the mail and cargo difficult, but in a few days everything of value was retrieved.

The Marine Board of Inquiry agreed with

Diver Lori Strohofer captures her exploration of the Hermes *on video. Photo: J. Cancelmo.*

The sergeant major, a type of damselfish, is easily recognized by its five vertical stripes. When guarding eggs, the sergeant major is extremely territorial and pugnacious. Photo: J. Cancelmo.

Captain Fernandez that an unusually strong southwesterly current had been pushing him faster than he had calculated for quite some time, and that weather conditions made land sightings impossible. The entries in Captain Fernandez's patent log were all up to date and reasonable, so he was exonerated of any negligence or wrongdoing in connection with the sinking.

The Dive. The *Caraquet* now lies in 40 feet (12 m) of water, 10 miles (16 km) due north of Bermuda. Six decades of exposure to the elements left their mark on this once-proud steamer. She is broken in several pieces and the wreckage is strewn for more than 100 yards (91 m). The enormous boilers lie intact, as do the heavy-duty capstans and winches. Giant-bladed propellers, bearings and disconnected sections of propeller shaft lie in disarray.

Vigilant patrols of sergeant majors and rainbow-colored wrasses are in constant motion over the twisted remains of the *Caraquet.*

A giant anchor amidst the wreckage marks the final remains of the Caraquet. *Photo: J. Cancelmo.*

The once powerful drive system of the Cristobal Colon, *now encrusted with marine life, lies motionless on the ocean floor. Photo: J. Cancelmo.*

2. MADIANA

DEPTH:	40 FEET (12 M)
SUNK:	1903
TYPE:	PASSENGER LINER
LENGTH:	ABOUT 345 FEET (105 M)

History. The British passenger steamer *Madiana*, captained by Roderick Frazer, was bound for Bermuda from New York, carrying passengers and a general cargo. As the *Madiana* approached Bermuda on the evening of Valentine's Day 1903, the captain tried to make sense out of the light he saw on land. He knew that the brightest light was either the lighthouse at Gibb's Hill, or the one at St. David's. The light, however, didn't exhibit any of the flashes characteristic of a lighthouse. Instead, it was a fixed, faint-to-moderate glow that seemed to waiver with intensity. Captain Frazer decided the light was St. David's, altered course, and crashed onto the reef just west of North Rock.

What he did not know at the time was that an accident had destroyed some of the reflectors and partially damaged the revolving mechanism in the Gibb's Hill Lighthouse. Despite the faulty equipment and the lack of repairs—the lighthouse had been malfunctioning for over a year—the Marine Board of Inquiry found Captain Frazer guilty of negligence. Later the ruling was overturned by the British Board of Trade.

The Dive. Since the *Caraquet* and *Madiana* are only one-half mile apart, they are usually explored as a two-tank dive. There are few spots on the *Madiana* deeper than 30 feet (9 m), thus allowing ample bottom time to explore the wreck and the many sand alleys that surround the site. The *Madiana* is close to the main reef line, which makes this an especially colorful dive. Visibility on the *Madiana* tends to be excellent, averaging between 80 (24 m) and 100 feet (30 m), and occasionally exceeding 200 feet (61 m). Guides are only needed for novices on this shallow, protected wreck.

3. CRISTOBAL COLON

DEPTH:	25-55 FEET (8-17 M)
SUNK:	1936
TYPE:	PASSENGER LINER
LENGTH:	499 FEET (151 M)

History. One of the most mysterious stories in the annals of Bermuda shipwreck history is the tale of the *Cristobal Colon.* The *Cristobal*, the largest wreck off Bermuda, ran aground on the northern reefs on October 25, 1936. She was a Spanish luxury liner, bound from Spain to Vera Cruz, Mexico. Crew members later stated that en route to Mexico, the vessel was taken over by a special committee which redirected the destination to Havana on orders from the Spanish Government.

In the fall of 1936, Spain was wracked by civil war and the Loyalists were about to lose control to the rebels. When the *Cristobal* struck the north reefs, she carried no passengers but had a suspiciously large crew of 160 persons, including 6 stewardesses. It is thought today that the vessel was sent to Cuba to pick up a shipment of arms for the Loyalists, as well as to smuggle some people out of Spain in a time of crisis. If that was the case, it was unsuccessful because the liner never reached Havana, and three months after the mishap the crew was returned to Spain.

Mystery still surrounds the final voyage of the coral-encrusted Cristobal Colon. *Was the Spanish passenger liner on a mission for the Loyalists during Spain's civil war when she sank off Bermuda? Photo: M. Strohofer.*

Negligence is suspected as the cause for grounding of the *Cristobal*. The wireless operator was listening to a broadcast from Madrid at the time of the accident, and it was the first voyage in five years for the ship's captain, Crescencia Navarro Delgado.

Almost 500 feet (152 m) long, with an unloaded weight of almost 11,000 tons (10,000 MT), the *Cristobal Colon* was handsomely outfitted, and many Bermudian homes are today adorned with her artifacts. Most were acquired when the salvage was auctioned in the Town of St. George's in March 1941.

The Dive. The *Cristobal Colon* now lies in 25 to 55 feet (8-17 m) between North Rock and the North East Breakers, about 8 miles (13 km) northeast of Dockyard. The queen of Bermuda shipwrecks plays hostess to a myriad of marine life, including occasional pelagic fish that wander in from the deep. Many big grouper, chubs, barracuda and sharks are often sighted here.

The *Cristobal* is broken into two main sections split by a sturdy reef line. Divers will find a considerable amount of wreckage on either side of this natural barrier. Crossing the reef, however, can be tricky, so it is suggested that divers interested in visiting both sides should ask for a guide. Being the largest wreck in Bermuda, there is plenty to keep divers occupied on either side of the reef. It is almost impossible to tour the entire wreck on a single dive. Some points of interest include: eight boilers scattered on both sides as well as on top of the reef, two massive propellers and shafts, numerous winches, gears, and stack mounts. The run to the wreck site is about an hour, but the dive is more than worth the trip.

Among the twisted wreckage, the long propeller shafts of the Cristobal Colon *are easily recognizable. Boilers, winches and stack mounts can also be found on the wreck. Photo: J. Cancelmo.*

Besides iron cannons, there are bronze slave bangles (manillas), as well as glass trading beads on the wreck. Photo: M. Strohofer.

4. MANILLA

DEPTH:	15-20 FEET (5-6 M)
SUNK:	ABOUT 1750
TYPE:	UNKNOWN
LENGTH:	UNKNOWN

History. The history of this wreck is sketchy. To confuse the issue further, in 1938 a cruise ship, the *Prince David,* ran aground on the same reef. It was able to free itself when the tide changed, but in the interim the passengers partied heartily, throwing many discarded beverage containers overboard (environmental concerns being somewhat lax in those days). This mixes up the exact dating of pottery shards and glass retrieved from the site today. Best guess is that the *Manilla* sank about 1750, and from the ordinance aboard, was probably under Dutch command. The make and length of the boat has never been determined, but one thing is almost certain: it was a "blackbirder," or slave trader. This can be deduced from the heavy armaments and bronze slave bangles discovered on the site. These bangles, or manillas, are what gives the unknown wreck her name. There are also a variety of glass beads strewn about the location, the same type that were used historically to trade for slaves.

The Dive. The estate of late Bermudian Harry Cox owns the salvage rights to the *Manilla* wreck, and it is officially off limits to commercial dive operations. Divers can visit the wreck site from private boats however. The numerous large iron cannons are the signature of this impressive ambassador of days long past, lining the western side of the North East Breakers.

The reefs surrounding the *Manilla* are some of the loveliest in Bermuda, being punctuated with small caverns, overhangs and swim-

Fire coral is characterized by a mustard brown to creamy white color. Not actually a coral, a brush against this hydrozoan can result in a painful, itchy rash. Photo: J. Cancelmo.

The coral-clad bow of the Taunton *points skyward on a sunny Bermuda afternoon. Photo: M. Strohofer.*

throughs. An extremely shallow site, divers rarely find themselves deeper than 20 feet (6 m). On windy days this creates a good deal of back and forth surge, but exhaustion can be avoided if one goes with the motion instead of trying to fight it.

5. TAUNTON

DEPTH:	10-40 FEET (3-12 M)
SUNK:	1920
TYPE:	CARGO STEAMER
LENGTH:	228 FEET (69 M)

History. Built in Copenhagen in 1902, the *Taunton*, under Norwegian registry and carrying a load of coal, was steaming from Norfolk, Virginia to St. George's when she met her demise.

The weather was misty on February 24, 1920 when the master of the *Taunton*, Captain Olsen, knowing they were getting close to Bermuda, posted a lookout. It was to no avail, however, because the 229-foot (69 m) *Taunton* ran hard aground on the North East Breakers.

The Dive. The *Taunton* is about equidistant from the *Cristobal* and *Aristo*, and with its shallower depth, makes a perfect second dive. Her bow section is exceptionally pretty. Pointed up at a slight angle, it comes to within ten feet (3 m) of the surface. Of particular interest is a Victorian style head still in place in the bow section. Apart from her engine and boilers, the hull from midships to stern has collapsed.

6. IRISTO (ARISTO)

DEPTH:	15-50 FEET (5-15 M)
SUNK:	1937
TYPE:	FREIGHTER
LENGTH:	250 FEET (78 M)

History. Less than a year after the *Cristobal Colon* ran up on the northern reefs, another vessel shared the same fate. This mishap was due in part to the *Cristobal* shipwreck.

The 250-foot (78 m) Norwegian steamer *Iristo*, captained by Christian Stephensen, left St. John's, Newfoundland on March 11, 1937. She was bound for Bermuda with a general cargo that included 200 barrels of gasoline, a fire engine and a steamroller.

On Monday, March 15, the *Iristo* sighted North Rock and took a bearing. Captain Stephensen also sighted the wreck of the *Cristobal*, but believed she was underway and heading seaward.

In order to clear the *Cristobal*, he ordered the *Iristo* turned. Unfortunately, she ran aground on the nearby Curlew Boiler. Later that day, a tugboat towed the *Iristo* off the reef but she quickly began taking in water and was towed back to the reef. The next morning, aided by more pumps, another attempt was made to tow the stricken vessel to St. George's Harbour. The rescue effort succeeded in pulling the *Iristo* one-half mile (.8 km) east of the North East Breakers where her bow plunged beneath the surface and the 2,950-ton (2,682 MT) freighter sank in 50 feet (15 m) of water.

The Marine Board of Inquiry charged Captain Stephensen with grave negligence for three

Nancy Stevens-Hands, Bermuda's official diving officer, inspects the forward winch on the bow of the Iristo. *Photo: M. Strohofer.*

The beacon at North Rock warns mariners of the dangerous boiler reefs that have sent many ships to the bottom. Photo: J. Cancelmo.

The foureye butterflyfish has a second set of "eyes" which confuses predators. Photo: J. Cancelmo.

Grooved braincoral has highly convoluted valleys and a groove that forms a double ridge. Photo: J. Cancelmo.

reasons: there were no large-scale charts of Bermuda on board; the bearing taken on North Rock was faulty; and, finally, he had no knowledge that the *Cristobal Colon* was wrecked, although that information had been published as early as November 28, 1936, in the *Notice to Mariners Bulletin*. Captain Stephensen had failed to familiarize himself with the waters around Bermuda.

To prevent another ill-prepared skipper from making the same mistake, the Board recommended that the funnel and at least one mast be removed from the *Cristobal Colon*.

The Dive. The *Iristo's* bow section rises to within 15 feet (5 m) of the surface. Unlike many shipwrecks in Bermuda, the *Iristo* is still very much intact. At midship, the engine and boilers are visible as is the propeller shaft running to the stem. The prop itself sits upright with one blade broken off at the hub.

Other points of interest include two large anchors and the remnants of the fire engine she was transporting. Due to the wreck's cohesive layout and the good visibility of the North East Breakers, divers with only a moderate amount of experience can safely dive the *Iristo* without a guide. This wreck is considered by many to be one of the best in Bermuda.

7. THE *BEAUMARIS CASTLE* AND THE *COLONEL WILLIAM BALL*

DEPTH:	30-40 FEET (9-12 M)
SUNK:	1873
TYPE:	CARGO (SAIL)
LENGTH:	202 FEET (61 M)
DEPTH	30-40 FEET (9-12 M)
SUNK:	1943
TYPE:	HARBOR BOAT
LENGTH:	119 FEET (36 M)

Certain reefs around Bermuda are more dangerous than others. The North Rock region as well as the Western Blue Cut area and the Club Heads waters are scattered with numerous shipwrecks. About 3 miles (5 km) northeast of Bermuda lies another reef that has bruised more than its share of hulls over the

The Beaumaris Castle, *an iron sailing vessel, ran aground on Mills Breaker in 1873. Three other wrecks lie within swimming distance of the* Beaumaris Castle. *Photo: J. Cancelmo.*

years. This area is known as Mills Breaker. Contrary to its name, Mills Breaker does not always break the surface. At high tide, without much wind, the sea surface over the reef appears as calm as if the water was a mile (2 km) deep.

Situated right off St. David's Lighthouse, the guiding light for sailors approaching Bermuda from the east, Mills Breaker is in a high traffic spot which compounds the formula for disaster. Two vessels that fell victim to this scenario were the *Beaumaris Castle* and the *Colonel William Ball*. They now rest within 40 yards (37 m) of each other at a maximum depth of 40 feet (12 m).

History. The more recent of the two wrecks, the *Colonel William Ball* was a 130-foot (39 m) luxury yacht built in 1929 as the *Egeria*. During World War II, she was commissioned as an army harbor boat. On January 29, 1943, the *Colonel William Ball*, captained by Fred A. Anderson, was towing a target to the north of Bermuda when the weather began to deteriorate. Due to 40-knot winds and poor sea conditions, the exercise was aborted. While returning to St. George's, the *Ball* collided with Mills Breaker. The engine room flooded, preventing the *Ball* from backing off the reef.

After being surveyed the next day, the harbor boat was declared a total loss. The army set up an inquiry into the mishap, and it was discovered that the conspicuous marker buoy warning mariners of the shallow water in the area had become detached several days earlier and was never replaced.

The *Beaumaris Castle* was an iron sailing vessel constructed in England almost 100 years before the *Colonel William Ball* sank. She was en route from Calcutta, India, with a cargo of linseed oil, jute and gum when she ran aground on Mills Breaker on April 25, 1873.

The initial survey concluded that the ship could be salvaged, but after three attempts and the death of a diver while trying to remove cargo, the efforts were dropped.

Used to secure the rigging on the Beaumaris Castle, *these deadeyes are made of lignum vitae, a very hard, heavy type of wood. Photo: J. Cancelmo.*

The Dive. Today the *Colonel William Ball* lies at a right angle to the *Beaumaris Castle*. Only a submerged, shallow breaker separates the two wrecks from each other, yet they are easy to tell apart because they are distinctly from different eras.

The *Beaumaris Castle* sits atop Mills Breaker with her bow in a sand hole 40 feet (12 m) deep. Her skeleton-like frame crisscrosses along the northeast side of the breaker. On top of the reef, two rows of deadeyes lie on their sides, suggesting the original beam of the vessel. Just over 200 feet (61 m) long, the *Beaumaris Castle* is the most interesting and photogenic shipwreck on Mills Breaker.

Schools of snapper repose in the shade of the many coral overhangs, while barracuda continually circle the surrounding breakers. Groupers can be found tucked away in dark corners and trumpetfish are always trying to disguise themselves in the gorgonians.

Visibility on the breaker can be limited, averaging between 40 and 60 feet (12 and 18 m). Diving these wrecks, however, is still phenomenal.

Besides the *Colonel William Ball* and the *Beaumaris Castle*, there are two more wrecks on Mills Breaker. One is thought to be the *Avenger*, a sailing vessel that sank in 1894. The other remains unidentified. Divers can swim in any direction for 100 yards (91 m) from the breaker and encounter wreckage of some sort.

Caution. When crossing over the breakers, the surge close to the surface can be powerful.

8. *RITA ZOVETTA*

DEPTH:	20-70 FEET (6-21 M)
SUNK:	1924
TYPE:	CARGO STEAMER
LENGTH:	350 FEET (106 M)

History. Bound for Baltimore, Maryland, from Gibraltar with a cargo of manganese ore, the Italian registered *Rita Zovetta* ran aground off St. David's Island on February 11, 1924.

At the time, Captain Fortunat de Gregari was trying to follow a Bermuda pilot boat into St. George's Harbour in heavy weather. Somehow

The Rita Zovetta *ran aground while following a pilot boat into St. George's Harbour. Bad weather and confusion about which lights the pilot boat was showing led to the accident. Photo: J. Cancelmo.*

Lying among the wreckage of the Rita Zovetta, an Italian cargo steamer which sank in 1924, are the rusted remains of her engine. Photo: J. Cancelmo.

he misread the pilot boat's lights and positioned the *Rita* on the wrong side of the channel where she ran aground.

Because of the inclement weather and confusion as to which lights the pilot boat was showing, the Marine Board of Inquiry acquitted Captain Gregari of any negligence. No lives were lost and the cargo was salvaged.

The Dive. Today the wreckage of the *Rita Zovetta* begins at 20 feet (6 m) and reaches a maximum depth of 70 feet (21 m). Divers can swim through the engine shaft housing and view the boilers and condensers, stacked on top of each other like huge iron building blocks. The intact stern of the *Rita* is by far the most interesting part of the wreck. Giant hull plates are still found standing here, supporting fragile decking. Her huge propeller is wedged against the reef, with two blades sheared off, testifying to the titanic impact with the reef.

Caution. Although an enchanting dive, this wreck demands a guide for all but the most experienced wreck divers. The *Rita's* numerous tunnels and gullies lead to dead ends, deeper water, or both. In addition, swimming under and through certain parts of the wreckage is not safe. The most important reason for a guide is the long swim from the stern of the *Rita* to where the dive boats must anchor. The entire wreck of the *Rita Zovetta* lies on the outside, or seaward side of the reef, where anchorage is usually impossible. If divers cannot find one of the few cuts through the reef, then the only exit is a long exhausting swim across the reef.

TEDDY TUCKER—PIONEER TREASURE HUNTER

Edward B. (Teddy) Tucker is one of the world's foremost treasure hunters and a recognized authority on maritime history. He has worked on projects with the National Geographic Society and the Smithsonian Institute, and served as a consultant for the National Science Foundation and the Soviet Academy of Sciences. Teddy has been featured in Life magazine, National Geographic, the Saturday Evening Post, the Paris Match, and numerous books and other magazines worldwide.

During World War II, Tucker tested dive gear and did underwater salvage for the Royal Navy. After the war, he returned to Bermuda and entered the commercial diving business doing island-wide underwater search and recovery work. It was the Spanish ship *San Pedro*, which Tucker discovered in 1950, that got him started in a career of treasure hunting. He worked this 16th century wreck for seven years finding silver coins, gold ingots, pearl buttons, and one of the most valuable single pieces of jewelry from a wreck in modern times—the famous emerald-studded gold cross. Later, while on display at the Bermuda Aquarium, this prized artifact was stolen and never recovered. Tucker found more than a hundred other shipwrecks around Bermuda. Many were spotted using a helium balloon.

Tucker's fame goes beyond shipwrecks. He has participated in several deep-ocean projects and in the 1970s was credited with the discovery of the six-gill shark in Bermuda waters. Teddy is also a founding member of the Bermuda Underwater Exploration Institute.

9. PELINAION

DEPTH:	20-30 FEET (6-9 M)
SUNK:	1940
TYPE:	CARGO STEAMER
LENGTH:	385 FEET (117 M)

History. The *Pelinaion* was a Greek steamer built in 1907. On December 22, 1939, the ship left Takiradi, a British port in West Africa, bound for Baltimore, Maryland with a large cargo of manganese ore. She was not scheduled to stop in Bermuda, but with the fuel supply running dangerously low, Captain Janis Valikas decided to make landfall in Bermuda to restock.

On the night of January 16, 1940, the 385-foot (117 m) *Pelinaion* entered Bermudian waters. The Captain, however, thought he was still twelve hours from the islands. Captain Volikas did not know that St. David's Lighthouse was blacked out for the war effort, and saw no signal lights before he ran aground a mile (1.6 km) from Cooper's Island, near St. David's.

Although in command of the *Pelinaion* for only 10 months, Captain Volikas had 24 years experience as a sea captain at the time of the accident. At the inquiry, he stated that an abnormal current must have been pushing his vessel faster than he and his officers had calculated. The Marine Board of Inquiry exonerated Captain Volikas of any negligence.

The Dive. The *Pelinaion* is one of the largest and most spectacular shipwrecks in Bermuda. She lies split over a reef at an angle of about 40

The now silent reciprocating steam engine on the Pelinaion *once powered the mighty freighter around the world. Photo: M. Strohofer.*

The Pelinaion *has several open areas allowing divers to swim safely through the wreck. Photo: J. Cancelmo.*

degrees to starboard. The bow section is at 30 feet (9 m) on the shallower side of the reef. The stern hits the sand at 70 feet (21 m). Two of the four boilers lie atop the reef, next to the engine, while the other two are in the sand. Other highlights of the wreck include four winches, a spare anchor and propeller on the aft-deck, the cargo hold ladder, and anchor chain by the ton.

An especially intriguing feature of the *Pelinaion* is the 15 feet (5 m) of water between parts of her hull and the sand which enable divers to easily swim under the wreck as they explore the area. Although the wreck is not strewn over a great distance, a guide is recommended so that key points are not overlooked. The dive is further accented by the many tunnels and caves in the reef line.

At night and on dark days coral
polyps open to feed on the
zooplankton being swept along by
the current. Photo: M. Strohofer.

Yellow and red encrusting sponges
are prolific under coral ledges and
just inside the entrances to caverns
along the shoreline of Harrington
Sound. Photo: J. Cancelmo.

10. *KATE*

DEPTH:	45 FEET (14 M)
SUNK:	1878
TYPE:	CARGO STEAMER
LENGTH:	200 FEET (61 M)

History. The *Kate* was a 200-foot (61 m) English Barkentine rig with an iron propeller bound for Le Harve, France, from Galveston, Texas. According to some accounts, the *Kate* ran aground at Long Bar, west of Bermuda, and was being towed to safety when she started sinking. She was deliberately run up on a reef for easy salvaging and repairs.

In a letter to the Royal Gazette, however, Captain William Simpson, master of the *Kate*, told a different story. He contended that the *Kate* did not run aground at Long Bar, "or any other bar," but hit some piece of flotsam and began taking on water.

The following dawn, December 1, 1878, he entered into a haggling debate with the pilot of the steam tug *Ackerman* over the cost of a tow. After a price was agreed upon, the *Ackerman*

Co-author Mike Strohofer fins towards the Kate's *towering propeller blade that hasn't moved in more than 100 years. Photo: J. Cancelmo.*

A member of the sea bass family, this coney measures about 12 inches (31 cm) in length. Photo: J. Cancelmo.

towed the *Kate* onto the reefs off Tucker's Town Beaches, contrary to Captain Simpson's wishes. The captain stated that his vessel would have made it to St. George's Harbour if his instructions had been followed.

The Marine Board of Inquiry did not agree with the frustrated Captain Simpson and his certificate was revoked for 6 months, beginning December 24, 1878. All crew members were saved and so were most of the 3,500 bales of cotton she was carrying.

The Dive. The wreck now lies at a maximum depth of 45 feet (14 m). Of particular interest is the odd-shaped, angular propeller, resting in 20 feet (6 m) of water atop the reef. An old-fashioned anchor sits exposed and upright on the reef. Her propeller shaft, boilers, winches and engine are also intact.

It takes only about a half-hour to explore the entire wreck site so most divers still have plenty of air to view the reef on the shore side of the *Kate*. Usually in residence are coneys, trumpetfish, bluehead wrasses, filefish, trunkfish and several species of damselfish. Brain and fungus corals, sea rods, sea fans and corky sea fingers also abound.

Being a much visited dive site, the fish are friendly and like to be fed. This is a good spot for fish portrait photography, and the wreck makes a terrific backdrop.

SOUTHERN WRECKS

11. *POLLOCKSHIELDS*

DEPTH:	20-30 FEET (6-9 M)
SUNK:	1915
TYPE:	STEAMER
LENGTH:	323 FEET (98 M)

History. The *Pollockshields* was originally a German vessel, built in Hamburg in 1890. Captured by the British early in World War I, the *Pollockshields* was sailing under the English flag with a cargo of munitions when she was wrecked during a hurricane on Bermuda's south shore, September 7, 1915. Five days before reaching her intended destination in Bermuda, en route from Cardiff, Wales, the storm hit. Captain Earnest Boothe changed the course of the 2,800-ton (2,546 MT) steamer to the south of Bermuda, intending to ride out the storm. Dead reckoning put the *Pollockshields* 80 miles (129 km) south of the islands. The driving rain and sea spray cut the visibility to less than 100 yards (91 m) and by the time the crew saw the

SPANISH GALLEONS

For nearly two hundred years, Spanish and Portuguese sailors dared the Caribbean hurricanes, hull-shattering reefs and Jamaican pirates in order to deliver the gold and silver treasure of the New World to Spain. The return route took the Spanish fleets through the perilous Florida straits and up the coast until the Gulf Stream turned east towards the deadliest landmark of them all, Bermuda, with its treacherous shallow reefs. Though few landfalls were attempted, storms and bad visibility claimed a number of Spanish Galleons.

Today, only piles of ballast stones mark the remains of the *San Pedro* (1594), the *Santa Ana* (1605), and the *San Antonio* (1621). Their treasure and valuable artifacts were salvaged in the 1950's by Bermudian treasure hunter, Teddy Tucker. Since only scant traces of wreckage remain, dive operators do not frequent these sites.

Robert Marx, a well-known treasure diver, believes there are still 12 undiscovered treasure wrecks in Bermuda waters.

These old clay pipes, bottles and other artifacts were found near Dockyard over 20 years ago. Removal of artifacts in Bermuda is prohibited and diving off Dockyard is no longer permitted. Photo: J. Cancelmo.

The English steamer Minnie Breslauer *sank on her maiden voyage in 1873. Photo: J. Cancelmo.*

reefs, it was too late to avert a collision.

The scene of the disaster, off Elbow Beach, became a theater for a daring sea rescue. The *Pollockshields's* distress signal brought guests out of the South Shore Hotel (now the Elbow Beach Surf Club). The guests quickly called for help which arrived in the form of an oldtime whaling man named Antonio Marshall. He figured that he could get a sturdy whale boat out through the surf and reach the *Pollockshields*, which remained on the reef. Four hundreds yards (366 m) is a long way in a hurricane, but after several stout attempts, the small boat pushed through 400 yards (366 m) of roiling surf and reached the stricken vessel. It took five trips to bring the crew of 34 and 7 cats to safety. The only fatality was the ship's captain who was swept overboard and drowned early in the rescue proceedings.

From 1915 to 1960, the *Pollockshields* sat on the reef, giving mute testimony to the power of an Atlantic hurricane. In August of 1960, after the wreck had been declared a menace to navigation, Teddy Tucker, a Bermuda diving pioneer, was commissioned to dynamite the wreck.

The Dive. The wreckage now lies in 20-30 feet (6-9 m) of water equally distributed on either side of the reef that sank the *Pollockshields*. To see both sides, divers must time their reef crossing with the surge.

Items of interest on this munition wreck include the huge brass shell casings and projectiles cemented into the reef. These armaments are unstable and should not be disturbed. Due to the surge, visibility tends to be reduced, averaging between 50 and 75 feet (15 and 23 m).

Except for the Grotto Bay barges, the *Pollockshields* is the only wreck in Bermuda accessible from shore. The local operator offers "scooter dives" to the wreck and surrounding reef.

Caution. Although guides are not needed to dive the *Pollockshields*, divers should be aware of the constant surge at the site, which can throw divers against wreckage. It is especially strong on a windy day or at extremely low tide.

12. MINNIE BRESLAUER

DEPTH:	40-70 FEET
	(12-21 M)
SUNK:	1873
TYPE:	STEAMER
LENGTH:	300 FEET (91 M)

History. On New Year's day in 1873, the English steamer *Minnie Breslauer* suffered the ignominious fate of sinking on her maiden voyage. En route from Lisbon, Portugal, to New York with a cargo of dried fruit, wine, cork and lead, her master, intending to use Bermuda as a landmark, approached too close and collided with a reef. Captain Peter Corbett tried to back the 300-foot (91 m) freighter off, but the damage was more severe than originally thought and the inrushing water soon sunk the ship. All 24 crew members survived.

Not all of the *Minnie* was salvaged by the B.W. Walker & Company, the agents for the shipping line. Ten days after the sinking, they took out a newspaper advertisement warning that anyone found in possession of cargo from the ship would be prosecuted. Bermuda's traditions die hard it seems, as other "midnight" salvors were at work.

The Dive. The *Minnie Breslauer* now lies in 40 to 70 feet (12-21 m) of water between Horseshoe Bay and Warwick Long Bay. A boiler sits upright against the reef, dividing the wreck in half. The bow section lies collapsed in the sand yet is easily recognizable. The stern section is overgrown with coral and is now part of the reef. Since there are no dangerous breakers close by, dive boats can anchor right over the wreck.

Besides the boiler, divers will want to swim along one of the stacks in the sand and explore the many inviting openings in the wreck. A school of goatfish is always in residence, and on the end of the bow section is a colony of black coral (do not touch!). Experienced wreck divers will not need a guide. Visibility varies considerably, but averages between 60 to 80 feet (18-24 m).

13. HERMES

DEPTH:	75 FEET (33 M)
SUNK:	1985
TYPE:	STEAMER
LENGTH:	165 FEET (50 M)

History. The *Hermes*, also called the *Fogo Brava*, is presently one of the most popular wreck dives in Bermuda. Technically, she is not a shipwreck at all, but was scuttled for the

The once proud Minnie Breslauer *now lies on a south shore reef near Horseshoe Bay. Photo: J. Cancelmo.*

The freighter Hermes *being sunk to create an artificial reef in 1985. Photo: M. Strohofer.*

purpose of creating an artificial reef.

The *Hermes* is a 165-foot (50 m) freighter built in Pennsylvania in 1943. She was abandoned in Bermuda because the owners did not want to pay the refitting costs. The Bermuda Government thus became the new heirs and in turn donated the ship to the Bermuda Dive Association, who sank her about one-half mile (.8 km) off Warwick Long Bay on May 15, 1985.

The Dive. Sitting upright in a 75-foot-deep (23 m) sand hole, the *Hermes* is flanked by a reef portside. Many fish have already claimed the wreck as home, including schools of barracuda that can usually be seen circling her still vertical mast. The *Hermes* is the most penetrable of all Bermuda wrecks as all the hatches and doors were removed prior to sinking. Divers can easily tour the twin diesel, six cylinder engines, the cargo hold, the galley and the pilot house. Because of the depth, guides are advised. Other points of interest include the propeller and the Captain's quarters. The visibility on the *Hermes* averages between 75 and 100 feet (23-30 m) and occasionally reaches 200 feet (61 m).

14. *VIRGINIA MERCHANT*

DEPTH:	40 FEET (12 M)
SUNK:	1661
TYPE:	FREIGHTER (SAIL)
LENGTH:	80-100 FEET (24-30M)

History. The *Virginia Merchant* is the oldest shipwreck that is frequently visited. The main attraction, however, is not the wreck itself, but the lovely reef dubbed "sandy hole" which surrounds the wreck site. The vessel sank more than 300 years ago on March 26, 1661 and most of the wreckage has long since disintegrated or disappeared beneath the sand and reef.

Co-author Michael Strohofer mans the now inoperative winch controls on the Hermes. *Photo: J. Cancelmo.*

Sea anemones have microscopic stinging capsules that are used to catch prey. Photo: J. Cancelmo.

Bad weather caught the English freighter en route from Plymouth, England to Jamestown, Virginia and forced her into Bermuda's maze of reefs. She was carrying 179 passengers and a large cargo of general supplies for the settlers in the Colonies. Only ten passengers survived.

The Dive. A dramatic archway through the breaker separates the sandy hole from the deeper part of the reef. A school of gray snappers can usually be seen hanging in the shadow of the arch. On one side of the archway, the reef drops down to 40 feet (12 m) where ballast stones from the *Merchant* are strewn in the sand. Of the few visible remnants of the wreck are the ship's anchor and anchor chain. From time to time, the wave action will move the sand and expose a musket shot or sounding weight. The other side of the archway is between 15 and 25 feet (5-8 m) deep. Guides are recommended only for novice divers. Visibility is usually around 80 feet (24 m).

15. *KING*

DEPTH:	55 FEET (17 M)
SUNK:	1984
TYPE:	TUG
LENGTH:	65 FEET (20 M)

The still vertical mast of the Hermes *rises to within 10 feet (3 m) of the surface. Photo: J. Cancelmo.*

History. The tug boat *King* was the first ship in Bermuda scuttled to create a marine habitat to be viewed by scuba divers. She was later followed by the *Hermes* and the *Triton*.

A few years after the *King* arrived in Bermuda, her owner left the tug boat business and the vessel was converted to a salvage boat. The *King*, though, never did any salvage work and the 65-foot (20 m) craft was eventually purchased by South Side Scuba Ltd. She was sunk one-half mile (.8 km) offshore, a short ride from Blue Water Diver's shop at the Wyndham Resort and Spa

The Dive. The *King* now sits in 65 feet (20 m) of water, half on the reef and half in the sand. Her bow points out to sea. Although small, this wreck has a number of interesting features. Fully intact, divers can tour the pilot house and galley. Peering through the engine room door will reveal all there is to see. It is inadvisable to enter the room because of the confined space and the heavy layer of silt which reduces visibility when disturbed. Some other points of interest include a winch mounted on the stern

and, lying off the stern in the sand, a device designed to direct propeller wash downward to blow the overburden of sand off a wreck site.

The 15 minutes needed to inspect the tug boat leaves ample bottom time to explore the surrounding reef. Along the top of the reef at 50 feet (15 m) are an interesting series of grooves forming repetitive patterns.

About 35 yards (32 m) off the bow is a large sand hole that runs perpendicular to the boat. By following the reef on either side of this sand hole, an orientation of the site can be easily maintained. The sand hole is popular for its prolific production of shells. There are several big helmet conchs that move around the area. Other shells found in the area are tellins, cowries, tritons, flamingo tongues and scotch bonnets. This site also features the usual assortment of tropical fish and a thriving coral community. Visibility is good, averaging between 70 and 90 feet (21-27 m).

A member of the wrasse family, the Spanish hogfish features large canine teeth in the front of each jaw. Photo: J. Cancelmo.

16. *MARY CELESTIA*

DEPTH:	55 FEET (17 M)
SUNK:	1864
TYPE:	PADDLE WHEEL STEAMER
LENGTH:	225 FEET (68 M)

History. During the American Civil War,
Bermuda was a strategic point for funneling
supplies from Europe to the Confederate States.
In Bermuda, cargos brought in on large vessels
were transferred to small, fast steamers which
then attempted to run the Union naval
blockade of the Confederate ports. The *Mary
Celestia* was one of these blockade runners.

After several successful runs to Wilmington,
North Carolina, the *Mary Celestia* cleared port
on September 6, 1864. Though her destination
was listed as Nassau, she was actually headed
for Wilmington with a cargo of bacon, corned
beef, rifles and ammunition. En route from
Hamilton Harbour, the *Mary Celestia* headed
up the south shore, intending to drop off the
ship's owner and the local pilot at the foot of
Gibb's Hill. Suddenly, she struck a reef, even
though the local pilot was at the helm. Within
ten minutes, the *Mary Celestia* went to the
bottom. The only loss of life was the ship's
cook who went to retrieve something from his
room, despite orders to abandon ship.

The Dive. Today, the wreck lies in 55 feet

Huge schools of fish can often be seen swarming around Bermuda's reefs. Photo: M. Strohofer.

(17 m) of water in a large sand hole about a quarter mile (.4 km) south of the Wyndham Resort and Spa. Although much of the collapsed hull structure is buried in the sand, the two paddle wheels, the boiler, and various pieces of machinery are still visible.

Getting to the *Mary Celestia* from the dive boat is an adventure in itself. The wreck lies about a hundred yards (91 m) from the reef where the dive boats anchor, and the approach to the wreck is over some of the most spectacular coral on the south shore. Because of the reef formations through which a diver must pass to find the *Mary Celestia*, a guide is recommended. Visibility is highly variable, but is usually between 60 and 80 feet (18-24 m).

WESTERN WRECKS

17. *B-29 BOMBER*

DEPTH:	25 FEET (8 M)
SUNK:	1961
TYPE:	AIRPLANE
LENGTH:	99 FEET (30 M)

History. Given Bermuda's location and the military activity it has seen over time, it is not surprising that several military aircraft have crashed there over the years. Most of them have never been found.

Off of the west end of the island, one such casualty was a *B-29 Bomber* that crashed during a practice exercise in 1961. The mishap, which apparently was due to a fuel delivery problem, fortunately did not claim any lives as the crew had enough time to bail out. The Air Force was very quick to salvage the site without attempting to raise the craft, possibly indicating the presence of classified, or even top secret equipment aboard. The wreck is now broken apart and scattered over a wide area, but some parts, such as the propellers, fuselage and wings, are readily recognizable to the diver.

The Dive. Resting in only 25 feet (8 m) of water, far enough off shore where the visibility is consistently good, the *B-29 Bomber* is an excellent second or even third dive to the *Caesar* and *Blanche King.* On clear days the bright aluminum reflects the sun's rays, making the wreck seem more recent than its 1961 vintage. There is seldom much current to contend with on the site, and plenty of reef in every direction to explore, with the ample bottom time remaining after the wreck has been examined.

Note: The *Caesar* is covered in this section, whereas the *Blanche King,* not being a major wreck site, has been omitted. The *Blanche King* was an American-built schooner which sank in 1920.

18. *NORTH CAROLINA*

DEPTH:	40 FEET (12 M)
SUNK:	1880
TYPE:	BARQUE
LENGTH:	200 FEET (61 M)

History. Five miles (8 km) southwest of Bermuda, between Long Bar and Little Bar, is the wreck of an English sailing barque called the *North Carolina.* Little is known of the sinking because the Bermuda Colonial Legislature failed to renew the Marine Court of Inquiry Act. The Act gave the Governer the power to call for an investigation into marine

A propeller of the B-29 bomber forms a huge "X" marking the spot of its final resting place on a Bermuda reef. Photo: M. Strohofer.

Deadeyes, once used to secure the rigging of the North Carolina, *have remained intact for more than 100 years. Photo: J. Cancelmo.*

disasters. It lapsed December 31, 1879, the day before the *North Carolina* ran aground. This technicality was enough to prohibit an official investigation.

We do know that the *North Carolina* was a frequent visitor to Bermuda, using the islands as a stopover point between England and the United States. On January 1, 1880, the date of her last voyage, the *North Carolina* was leaving Bermuda bound for England with a cargo of cotton, bark and fuel. On the way out to sea, Captain Alexander Buchan ran the 200-foot (61 m) vessel aground. On the 27th, an attempt was made to refloat the barque, but when the ship's anchor crashed through her hull, the *North Carolina* sank permanently.

The Dive. A classic shipwreck by any standards, the *North Carolina* sits majestically on the bottom with her stern section 20 feet (6 m) deep and her bow lying at 40 feet (12 m).

Unusual for shallow water shipwrecks, the

bow is much more intact than the stern. Her 20-foot (6 m) bow sprit, totally coral-encrusted, rises gradually from 25 feet (8 m) to within 10 feet (3 m) of the surface, giving the illusion of a "ghost ship" forever underway. A row of deadeyes on either side of the hull add strongly to this impression. Although many shipwrecks off Bermuda contain deadeyes, none are as picturesquely intact as those on the *North Carolina*. She is one of the most photogenic wrecks in Bermuda.

Caution. The bottom is very silty and visibility will be quickly reduced if it is stirred up. Careless divers can easily ruin a dive for an entire group. When diving this wreck, it is a good idea to stay at least 4 feet (1.2 m) off the bottom. Novices are encouraged to have a guide because of the silt problem and because only a short distance from the wreck is much deeper water. On a good day, the visibility can range from 70 to 90 feet (21-27 m).

19. CAESAR

DEPTH:	25-35 FEET (8-11 M)
SUNK:	1818
TYPE:	BRIGANTINE
LENGTH:	UNKNOWN

History. Only four short years after her construction in 1814, this English brigantine struck a shallow reef southwest of Bermuda and joined the fleet of shipwrecks scattered around the reefs south of Chub Heads. En route from the British Isles to Baltimore, Maryland, Captain James Richardson's charts did not show Bermuda's Barrier Reef extending out as far as they did, and on May 17, 1818, he unwittingly sailed his vessel hard aground. The embarassed captain and crew all reached shore safely, and a salvage attempt was launched, but due to the mundane nature of her cargo, efforts were less than thorough. The *Caesar* was carrying kegs of white lead, bottles of various descriptions, bricks and an array of huge round grindstones.

Onboard the vessel at the time of her sinking was a special order consignment of flasks, destined not to be on hand for the gala celebration they were intended to enhance in the United States. These rare, one of a kind Mesonic and Melon flasks are of particular interest to the antique bottle collector.

The Dive. The exact length of the *Caesar* is unknown at this time, but it hardly matters

Giant grindstones, many stacked in two's or three's and weighing over a ton, litter the wreck of the Caesar. *Photo: J. Cancelmo.*

Parrotfish grazing on coral can actually be heard scraping away polyps and embedded algae. Photo: J. Cancelmo.

This hairy blenny, measuring less than 6 inches (15 cm), was photographed near the east end of Harrington Sound. Photo: J. Cancelmo.

nearly two hundred years later, since few traces are left of the wooden hull ship. The vessel was recently re-salvaged by Bermuda's wreck diving legend, Teddy Tucker, and he too chose to leave much of the cargo to the salty designs of the sea. Time has had little effect on the giant grindstones with the square holes in the centers. Many are still stacked in two's and three's, the 4-inch (100 mm) thick ones weighing over a ton each.

20. DARLINGTON

DEPTH:	15-30 FEET (5-9 M)
SUNK:	1886
TYPE:	STEAMER
LENGTH:	ABOUT 285 FEET
	(86 M)

History. The *Darlington*, an iron-screw steamer, was bound from New Orleans to Bremen, Germany, with a cargo of cotton and corn, products commonly exported from the southern states in the late nineteenth century. Early on February 22, 1886, Captain Richard Ward sighted the lighthouse at Gibb's Hill which he estimated to be 30 miles (48 km) away. He altered his course toward the light. A

Coral polyps are generally retracted during the day and open at night to feed. These clusters of flower coral extend long transparent tentacles at night to feed on plankton. Photo: J. Cancelmo.

closer look at the charts on board would have made clear that this course change was taking his ship right over Bermuda's western reefs. After about six miles (10 km) on the new course, the *Darlington* came to a grinding halt and stuck fast on the reef. Damage was too severe to refloat the steamer.

The Marine Board of Inquiry found the ship's master negligent and also cited the first mate for failure to keep a lookout when approaching an unknown coastline after being ordered to do so. Both men had their certificates of competency revoked for six months.

The Dive. The deepest of the *Darlington's* remains are at 30 feet (9 m) yet some parts of the wreck are in less than 15 feet (5 m) of water. Although most of the wreck is collapsed, her propeller shaft, winches, boilers and other large pieces of machinery are still visible and make for an interesting dive.

21. *L'HERMINIE*

DEPTH:	25 FEET (8 M)
SUNK:	1838
TYPE:	FRIGATE
LENGTH:	300 FEET (91 M)

History. Four miles (6 km) west of Ireland Island, between the outer reefs known as Chub Heads and Western Blue Cut lies what is left of the 60-gun French frigate *L'Herminie*. She was heading for Brest, France from Havana when inclement weather struck and her captain decided to seek shelter in Bermuda.

When land was sighted through the heavy seas, *L'Herminie* was already inside the reefs and, being a large vessel at 300 feet (91 m)

Flower coral is common on many reefs. Photo: M. Strohofer.

The Constellation *was made famous by the movie* The Deep. *Part of her cargo of cement bags are now solidified. Photo: J. Cancelmo.*

long, she lacked maneuverability. With no possible escape, the course change ordered by Captain Bazoche was mainly a decision of grounding the ship where she could be most easily salvaged. It was December 4, 1838 when the *L'Herminie* crashed into the reef. Her crew was put to shore safely and, in the days to follow, salvage operations were carried out.

The Dive. Her hull has long since broken up and disappeared beneath the sand, but twenty-five of her iron cannons are still visible today. Forged in Ruelle, France, the cannons are accompanied by a good assortment of cannon balls. One of the ship's winches lying in the sand is still recognizable. This site is easily silted up when divers closely inspect the cannons. On a good day, visibility is about 50 feet (15 m).

22. *CONSTELLATION*

DEPTH:	30 FEET (9 M)
SUNK:	1943
TYPE:	SCHOONER
LENGTH:	200 FEET (61 M)

History. The *Constellation* lies only 50 yards (46 m) east of the *Nola* and is probably the most talked about shipwreck in Bermuda. She was made famous by Peter Benchley's book *The Deep* which was later made into a movie, much of which was filmed in Bermuda. Commonly referred to as the "Woolworth's Wreck" by the local divers, the *Constellation* is still loaded with empty bottles, assorted glassware, ceramic tiles and the famous medical ampules—none of which contain morphine.

The ill-fated, four-masted schooner was

sailing from New York to La Guira, Venezuela, when she ran into rough weather in July, 1943. When the 200-foot (61 m) wooden vessel began taking on water, Captain Howard Neves attempted to navigate through the hazardous reefs around Western Blue Cut to reach refuge in Bermuda. The *Constellation* never made it. Instead, she sliced into a reef and sank.

The Dive. Besides the delicate medical supplies and glassware still found on the *Constellation*, the wreck is marked by hundreds of stacked cement bags, which were also part of her general cargo. These giant mounds are now rock hard. Other items of interest on the *Constellation* center around her varied cargo, which includes barrels of cold cream, bottles which housed everything from nail polish to mineral water, slate, windows, tile and china.

On a calm day, this is an ideal place for snorkelers. In some spots, the wreckage is less than 15 feet (5 m) deep and can be free-dived easily. The wreck site is teeming with fish life which can be hand-fed by snorkelers.

Because of the shallow depth and the proximity to the *Nola*, a diver can visit both wrecks on the same dive. The visibility is normally about 100 feet (30 m).

The unusually shaped trumpetfish is often found in a vertical position, imitating the elongated gorgonian sea whips. Photo: J. Cancelmo.

23. *LARTINGTON*

DEPTH:	20-35 FEET (6-11 M)
SUNK:	1879
TYPE:	FREIGHTER
LENGTH:	245 FEET (74 M)

History. Short Brothers, a shipbuilder in Sunderland, England, built the 878-ton (798 MT) freighter *Lartington* in 1875. She was 245 feet (74 m) long with a 32-foot (10 m) beam. Little is known about the early voyages of the *Lartington* other than she was owned by J.S. Barwick and made several Atlantic crossings.

Under the command of Captain George Dixon, the *Lartington* departed Savannah, Georgia on December 8, 1878 headed for Revel, Russia with a cargo of 4,000 bales of cotton. At sea for less than a day, the *Lartington* was hit by a southeasterly gale of such violence that the captain changed course and headed for the safety of Bermuda.

Unfortunately, the captain's good intentions turned for the worst. The *Lartington* ran into a

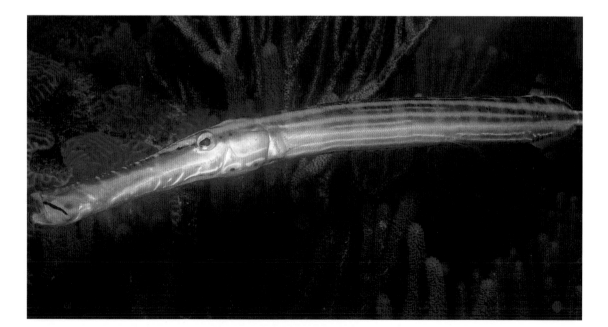

shallow reef inside the main barrier reef near Western Blue Cut on the morning of December 14. No lives were lost and all crew aboard were safely transported to Hamilton. But the Marine Board of Inquiry found Captain Dixon careless and negligent because he failed to take proper depth soundings.

The Dive. The *Lartington* rests at a depth of 25 feet (8 m) a few hundred yards (91 m) north of two other popular wreck dives—the *Constellation* and the *Montana*. Much of the 245-foot-long (74 m) vessel has been reduced to a scatter of flattened plates and rubble, but a portion of the ship's bow, her broken propeller blades, and her two boilers remain easy to recognize. The steam boilers that once powered the proud cargo vessel rise to within 10 feet (3 m) from the surface. The ship's name can still be read on the ship's twisted bow section. The site is basically a sand and rubble bottom, surrounded by large coral heads. Visibility during the summer months ranges from 50 to 75 feet (15-23 m). Winter clarity improves to 75 to 150 feet (23-45 m).

name that often persists today. Research clearly indicates, however, that this is the wreck of the *Nola*.

The Dive. The *Nola* sank on solid reef so her remains are not covered with sand, although most of the wreck is coral-encrusted. There is much to see on the *Nola* which is broken into three major parts, all in less than 30 feet (9 m) of water. The paddle wheels are easily recognizable as are the forward stack, boilers and piles of anchor chain. Although the bow is collapsed, the fantail stern section is still intact.

Dive boats can usually be seen on the *Nola* due to the ease of the dive and the excellent visibility which averages about 100 feet (30 m). The fish here are prolific, and is an ideal spot for photographers.

The remains of the Nola *(Montana), a Confederate blockade runner during the American Civil War, lie north-northwest of Ireland Island. Photo: J. Cancelmo.*

24. NOLA (MONTANA)

DEPTH:	30 FEET (9 M)
SUNK:	1863
TYPE:	PADDLE WHEEL STEAMER
LENGTH:	236 FEET (72 M)

History. The *Nola* was the first of two Civil War blockade runners to wreck on Bermuda's reefs, the second being the *Mary Celestia*. The 236-foot (72 m) paddle wheel steamer was scheduled to stop at Bermuda to load coal for a run to Wilmington, North Carolina. Following a rough passage across the Atlantic from Glasgow, Scotland, Captain William Rollins misjudged the channel at Western Blue Cut and put the ship on the reefs about 8 miles (13 km) north-northwest of Ireland Island.

All the cargo and crew were removed safely, but it was impossible to refloat the 750-ton (682 MT) vessel because of a ten-foot (3 m) gash in her hull. Somehow, over the years, the shipwreck was misnamed the *Montana*, a

CHAPTER VII   REFEFS

There are more than 600 square miles (968 sq km) of colorful reefs surrounding Bermuda. Every wreck described in this book has a nearby reef with an abundant variety of tropical fish and invertebrates. In addition to the wreck site, the fringing reef that encircles the island offers an almost endless number of dive sites.

The "boiler" or breaker reefs on the south shore and in the North Rock areas are especially dramatic dives. The frothy white foam, hence the name "boiler," is caused by the swells breaking over the shallow reefs. Many of Bermuda's boiler reefs are shaped like miniature atolls. The perimeter of the reefs project from the bottom to near the surface. Inside is a dished-out cavity which is a haven for a colorful assortment of invertebrates and fish.

25. SOUTH WEST BREAKER

DEPTH: 20-30 FEET (6-9 M)

One and a half miles (.8 km) off Church Bay on the south shore is the South West Breaker, a special spot frequented by most dive operators. At low tide, the reef boils white as the sea pounds against its exposed surface. The sheer sides of its 200-foot (61 m) perimeter drop to a maximum depth of 30 feet (9 m).

The highlight of the South West Breaker is a large cavern that penetrates through the middle of the reef. Pink and white sponges line its ceiling and walls. The entrance, located on the south face, begins at the base of the breaker and forms an archway wide enough for two divers to enter abreast. It quickly narrows, but midway through the reef the tunnel angles

upward and expands until it reaches the north opening. Here, banded coral shrimp can be found, and a resident 3-foot (.9 m) barracuda is often seen near the surface. The reefs surrounding the breaker thrive with dozens of tropical fish varieties. The purple seafans are spectacular and many are over 5 feet (1.5 m) high.

26. CATHEDRAL CAVERN

DEPTH: 30-60 FEET (9-18 M)

The most spectacular reef dive off the east end of the island is the Cathedral. Stumbled upon by accident in 1989, it has become the perfect complement on two-tank dive excursions to the *Pelinaion* or *Rita Zovetta*. Dive boats anchor just inside the reefline in a huge sand hole 30 feet (9 m) deep. From here it is only a short swim up and over the beginning of the main breaker line, and down into another cigar-shaped gully. The northeast corner of the gully appears to dead end, but looks are deceiving. About 10 feet (3 m) off the bottom there is a tunnel that leads straight through the reef. It is wide enough for only one diver at a time. The surge funnels through the tunnel, called the window by the locals, so you must time your kicks with the flow. You'll quickly shoot through and end up outside the reef.

Giant purple sea fans are in abundance on Bermuda's reefs. Like other gorgonian corals, their polyps feed on drifting zooplankton. Photo: J. Cancelmo.

Common to Bermuda's reefs, the corallimorphian can be found in clusters, often blanketing an entire side of a reef. Photo: J. Cancelmo.

The view from here is magnificent with the surf rhythmically breaking overhead, but it is only a preamble of what is to come. A left turn one outside the reef quickly reveals a prominent overhang which marks the cavern entrance. Once inside the enormous grotto, it is easy to see how it got its name. Light filters through the holes in the top of the reef, creating shafts of light, much like the effects of stained glass. The exit side can clearly be seen, a shimmering, silvery-blue, against the black of the interior. After a few moments your eyes will adjust to the reduction in light, and the short colorful sponges and purple algae can be seen lining the walls. Good buoyancy is required here because the substrate is quite powdery, and silting which can occur quickly lasts a long time. It is not usually a problem because there is 50 feet (15 m) of water to work with once inside the Cathedral.

Spiny lobsters and guinea chicks can be seen nesting inside the sharp coral crevices, and on the ledges adorning the sides of the cavern. A school of horse-eyed jacks is usually seen patrolling the ocean side entrance, and a large black grouper slowly moves off into the shadows as divers enter. From time to time, there is also a 200-pound (91 kg) jewfish which can be seen just outside the shore side, or what is usually the exit to the cathedral. In winter months 4- to 8-foot (1.2-2.4 m) tarpon frequent the site.

Caution. Stay with the guide because after you exit the cavern, there is a maze of tunnels and gullies leading every which way. It can be very difficult to find the boat without surfacing.

PRESERVATION OF CORAL REEFS

Coral reef formations are comprised of thousands of individual tiny coral polyps living as a community of animal life. Each tiny polyp is capable of independent existence, yet in actuality, the polyps within each colony are interdependent. Coral polyps feed on planktonic organisms that float by, but the majority of their nutrition comes from photosynthesis through a symbiotic relationship with internal microscopic algae.

The polyps are covered by a slippery substance secreted by the coral. This mucous protects the coral tissue and helps move sediment off the coral. When this layer of mucous is removed, the coral tissue is very vulnerable to a number of fouling organisms such as sponges and algae. There is a long list of predators and competitors of the coral polyp: the flamingo tongue, fireworm, butterflyfish, parrotfish, boring sponges and mollusks to name a few. Damage from any of these marine competitors is usually very localized. Destruction of coral reefs on a large scale can be caused by heavy storms, pollution or sedimentation.

A diver's impact on coral may be negligible when diving a reef area seldom frequented by divers. But reefs visited by a large number of divers can be adversely affected. Some marine biologists feel that the act of touching coral crushes living tissue and displaces the mucous covering, creating a perfect settling medium for competitor organisms. Proper buoyancy control is the key to minimizing diver damage to coral reefs. Enjoy the sights of the reef but always stay several feet away to prevent inadvertent damage.

CHAPTER **VIII** SNORKELING

Bermuda offers idyllic conditions for snorkeling enthusiasts. The shallow protective reef that completely surrounds the island reduces wave action and currents to a minimum, and allows easy snorkeling from all sides of the island. Extremely calm conditions prevail at the numerous coves and protected beaches along the south shore. In addition, many of the sites accessible only by boat are shallow enough to be enjoyed while snorkeling.

Masks, fins and snorkels can be rented at most of the beachside hotels. Safety flotation devices are also available and are recommended when snorkeling. For the novice, the dive operators can provide instruction.

Eastern Sites

27. TOBACCO BAY

Tobacco Bay is a popular public beach on the very edge of St. George's Parish. To get to this picturesque site, follow Duke of Kent Street up from the town of St. George's and go over the hill to the water.

Columns of rock 15 to 25 feet (5-8 m) high separate the bay from the ocean. Water depth in the bay averages less than 10 feet (3 m), but swim between the limestone boulders and you will be in the ocean. Immediately outside the rocks, the depth is about twice that of the bay. Swimming farther out to sea will provide deeper water, but it tends to be murky, so it is better to follow the coastline in either direction.

The bottom consists of rocks smoothed and rounded by eons of wave action. It is difficult for reef-building corals to get a good grip on these rocks. The result has been a proliferation of low-lying patch reefs, blanketing the seabed.

They are covered with a colorful sampling of Bermuda's ubiquitous soft corals. Sea hares, eels, octopus and sea horses can all be found along this rocky coast.

During the season, Tobacco Bay is equipped with public facilities where snorkeling gear can be rented and food can be purchased.

28. ACHILLES BAY

On the eastern tip of Bermuda, between Fort St. Catherine and Tobacco Bay, is Achilles Bay with its small secluded beach. To get there, take the main road leading to Fort St. Catherine. At the foot of the hill before the fort is a smaller road that leads to the bay. From the parking lot, it is only a short walk to the water. The area is very rocky and wet suit boots or sneakers are strongly advised.

A mere 30-yard (27 m) swim will take snorkelers outside the rocks to an expanse of patch reef heavily laden with corky sea fingers. Even when the polyps are not extended, they are always fuzzy. Conchs, which are protected by law, are often seen lying in the sand areas between the reefs. Deep water is a long distance from the beach, making this a good site for novices. Visibility averages between 60 and 80 feet (24 m).

The numerous shallow reefs in Bermuda offer snorkelers easy access to the underwater world. Photo: J. Cancelmo.

A close-up view of feeding coral polyps taken at night on the South West Breaker. Photo: M. Strohofer.

29. JOHN SMITH'S BAY

In addition to being a wonderful snorkeling site, John Smith's Bay is a popular spot for night diving. Located on the south shore, between Pink Beach and Watch Hill Park, John Smith's Bay is easy to find. It is just around the corner from Devil's Hole, another prominent landmark. The beach itself is long and scenic. Looking east, one will see Gurnet Rock in the distance, marking the entrance to Castle Harbour.

A quarter mile (.4 km) from the beach can be seen a constant boil of white water where the reef line breaks the surface. Snorkelers, however, need to swim only 50 yards (46 m) before encountering solid reef. These reefs, as beautiful as any in Bermuda, rise to within a few feet of the surface from a depth of 25 feet (8 m). There are many canyons and tunnels that can be seen from the surface. A school of large midnight parrotfish can always be seen patrolling these waters.

John Smith's Bay rivals Elbow Beach and Church Bay for the best snorkeling in Bermuda.

Expect a good deal of company when visiting this beach during the height of the season. Visibility is usually excellent, ranging from 80 to 100 feet (24-30 m).

CENTRAL SITES

30. SHELLY BAY

On calm summer days, Shelly Bay, between Flatt's Village and Crawl Hill on the north shore, is populated with swimmers, snorkelers and sun bathers. During windy, rough days, it becomes a windsurfer's paradise and the carnival-colored, triangular sails can be seen whistling along the coast.

Easy access to the water, coupled with the natural protection of the bay, makes this an

Sunsets enhance Bermuda's naturally stunning coastline. Photo: M. Strohofer.

Carpet anemones remain closed during the day. These were photographed at Little Reef. Photo: M. Strohofer.

Devonshire Bay, on Bermuda's south shore, offers a calm mooring for boats. Near the rocks on either side of the entrance to the Bay, snorkelers and divers can find a wide variety of marine life. Photo: M. Strohofer.

ideal snorkeling site. The water is shallow up to the reef about 50 yards (46 m) from the beach. Grunts, breams, lizardfish, peacock flounder and hogfish can be found on the reef as well as right off the beach.

Food service and beach rentals are available at this public beach during the season. The visibility is generally excellent, averaging between 80 and 100 feet (24-30 m).

Limestone cliffs fringe much of the Southampton shoreline. Photo: J. Cancelmo.

31. DEVONSHIRE BAY

A convenient little beach centrally located on the south shore, Devonshire Bay is often passed by unnoticed. Finding it, however, is easy. About a half-mile (.8 km) west of where Collector's Hill merges with the South Shore Road is Devonshire Bay Road. At the end of the road is the bay.

Beach and rocks surround the bay in an arc of about 270 degrees. The remaining 90 degrees are open to the sea. Due to this natural protection, there are usually boats moored in the bay so snorkelers and divers should use caution.

The bottom is primarily sand, which affords little protection for fish and other marine creatures. The mouth of the bay is where to find the action. The rocks on either side of the

The well camouflaged blue-striped
lizardfish is torpedo shaped.
Sometimes seen partially buried in
the sand, this species is more
commonly found propped up on its
ventral fins, ready to attack small
fish. Photo: J. Cancelmo.

The timid squirrelfish can normally
be found hiding under ledges or
overhangs during the day. Active at
night, their large eyes help them see
in low light. Photo: J. Cancelmo.

entrance are a good place to see fish, along with the characteristic variety of marine invertebrates. For those less venturesome, snorkeling along the sides of the bay will reveal an amazing amount of invertebrate life that make good subjects for macro photography. Visibility averages between 60 and 80 feet (18-24 m) and tends to be better closer to the mouth of the bay.

32. ELBOW BEACH

Elbow Beach is one of the best snorkeling spots in Bermuda that can be reached without a boat. It marks the east end of the famous south shore string of beaches that runs nearly 5 miles (8 km), ending at Church Bay on the west end. Along this stretch of the island exists one of the most scenic coastlines in the world. From most spots, the reef is within easy swimming distance for snorkelers.

At Elbow Beach, the reef begins only 10 yards (9 m) from shore and continues out to sea for over a mile (1.6 km). First-time snorkelers will be awestricken. Every kick of the fins will bring interesting and wonderful marine creatures into focus. The breakers farther offshore have an extensive labyrinth of tunnels and caves which are home to tarpon in the winter and horse-eyed jacks in the summer.

Elbow Beach has other attractions as well. It is the only location in Bermuda where a bona fide shipwreck can be reached by snorkeling from a public beach. A 300-yard (274 m) swim offshore will take one to the wreck of the *Pollockshields* which sank in 1915. Swimming leisurely, a veteran snorkeler can reach it in about 10 minutes. The wreck should only be explored by experienced free divers when the weather is calm. Flotation devices should be worn by everyone venturing that far out.

A word should be said about protocol at Elbow Beach. The beach front is divided into two sections. The beach directly in front of the hotel is private, while the beach to the west of the hotel is public. It is suggested that divers enter the water from the public beach to the west of the hotel and swim east to the Surf Club Restaurant. Directly in front of the restaurant is a conspicuous break in the reef line. Snorkeling through this gap will take skin divers right over the wreck. Visibility is variable, averaging between 50 and 75 feet (15-23 m).

Sea anemones are in the phylum Cnidaria, as are corals and jellyfishes. Photo: J. Cancelmo.

Warwick Long Bay is marked on its western tip by two large boulders just offshore of its half-mile (.8 km) long beach. Photo: M. Strohofer.

WESTERN SITES

33. WARWICK LONG BAY, JOBSON'S COVE, STONEHOLE BAY AND CHAPLIN BAY

Just east of Horseshoe Bay in Warwick Parish are found Warwick Long Bay, Jobson's Cove, Stonehole Bay and Chaplin Bay, separated from each other by only a few yards of rocky coastline.

The largest of the four beaches is Warwick Long Bay which is about a half-mile (.8 km) in total length. There are two huge boulders just offshore from the western tip of the bay that are highly visible from the road.

Not far from these two landmarks, and to the west, lies a small headland that divides

Warwick Long Bay from Jobson's Cove. A tiny secluded beach surrounded by rough ironshore (the black jagged limestone rock common to the Bermuda coast), Jobson's Cove is a marvelous place to slip away from it all. A small but steep embankment must be maneuvered in order to get from the sand path to the inlet. Jobson's Cove is nearly cut off from the open ocean, having only a narrow link to the sea. The maze of sand trails connecting these four beaches is commonly selected by horseback riders from the local riding stables as an exercise circuit.

Walk past a couple more rocks and ledges and Stonehole Bay appears. Conspicuous by its namesake, this site is marked by a giant hole eroded through the limestone rock that makes up the shoreline. Spectacular photos can be taken here using the natural gateway as the foreground and the pounding surf as the background. Stonehole Bay is about twice the size of Jobson's Cove and has a much larger beach area. When snorkeling from these inlets, be careful to stay clear of the rocks as they are sharp and easily capable of cutting unprotected skin.

To get a good perspective of the area, stand up on the South Shore Road and look down at the coast. This way it is easy to see the natural barriers that identify the various coves and inlets. Stonehole Bay and Warwick Long Bay are immediately noticeable from this vantage point. Looking over the rocks to the west, Horseshoe Bay can be seen in the distance. Except for Warwick Long Bay, the beaches are not individually marked.

The snorkeling in all these bays is generally excellent, with visibility averaging around 80 feet (24 m). Little fishing is done along this stretch of shoreline so there is a multitude of fish ranging from the tiniest wrasse to the massive grouper.

The last little beach in this fascinating stretch is Chaplin Bay. It is slightly larger than Stonehole Bay and has a natural curve to it that the other bays do not.

Stonehole Bay got its name from a giant hole eroded through the limestone rock. Photo: M. Strohofer.

Chaplin Bay is just one of the western bays where beautiful beaches can be found. Photo: M. Strohofer.

34. CHURCH BAY

Church Bay is located in Southampton just off the South Shore Road about three quarters of a mile (.4 km) west of the Wyndam Resort and Spa. The shoreline road hugs the coast high above the water, and the first turnoff approaching Church Bay from the east provides a spectacular view of the bay, the reefs, the beach, and the limestone cliffs. Church Bay is a public beach and there is a parking area and a paved, but steep, walkway down to the sand.

Snorkelers may enter the water anywhere along the beach. Under normal conditions,

The secluded beach at Jobson's Cove in Warwick provides easy access for snorkelers to enter the water. Photo: J. Cancelmo.

there are no breaking waves and the water is calm. A line of boiler reefs acts as a barrier and very amply protects Church Bay most of the time. Snorkelers will find these shallow reefs almost like natural aquariums that host colorful tropical fish, soft and hard corals, and a number of other interesting invertebrates. Caution should be exercised when there are ground swells breaking on the beach, or strong southerly winds.

35. SOMERSET LONG BAY

Somerset Long Bay is tucked away on the southwest end of Bermuda, not far from Daniel's Head. To get there, take the South Shore Road to the outskirts of Somerset, where Long Bay Road intersects from the south. Follow Long Bay Road to the water, where it makes a sharp right turn at Daniel's Head

THE BERMUDA AQUARIUM, MUSEUM AND ZOO

A stop at the aquarium is a good way to get acquainted with Bermuda's colorful marine life. The fascinating array of specimens range from parrotfish to sharks, and from sea horses to giant turtles. Integrated with the aquarium is a maritime museum, a children's zoo with monkeys, pink flamingos and an aviary of tropical birds. The museum is of special interest to divers with its display of shipwreck artifacts including valuable coins, jewelry, pottery and bottles. Also on display are rare seashells and works in Bermuda cedar by local craftsmen.

The aquarium, museum and zoo are located in the village of Flatts in Hamilton Parish. Telephone: 292-2727

Juvenile Spanish hogfish can be observed picking parasitic crustaceans off other fish using its pronounced set of front dentures. Photo: J. Cancelmo.

A member of the sea bass family, the butter hamlet can be recognized by the black blotch at the base of the tail and a blue-edged black spot on the snout. Photo: J. Cancelmo.

These purple tunicates are prolific in the shallows of Harrington Sound. The "sea squirt" tubes are approximately 1/2-inch (12.5 mm) long. Photo: J. Cancelmo.

Road. Stay on Long Bay Road until reaching the Somerset Nature Preserve. Somerset Long Bay is adjacent to the nature preserve.

The beach itself sits back from the road, but a sign is posted, and there is a parking lot and a lovely little picnic area overlooking the bay. The picnic tables are surrounded by tall, beautiful hibiscus and oleander hedges, adding a sweet, memorable scent to the fresh ocean air. In addition to being secluded, it is one of the most attractive picnic spots on the island.

By Bermuda standards, the bay is large. The beach runs for about 100 yards (91 m) and the water remains shallow for approximately 100 yards (91 m). This makes it an excellent snorkeling site for novices. Veteran skin divers might find this site a bit slow due to the relatively shallow water and the lack of a solid reef structure. Visibility is usually variable, ranging between 70 and 100 feet (21-30 m).

36. BERMUDA SNORKEL PARK

Ideal for beginners, the Bermuda Snorkel Park at Dockyard has beach rentals and accommodates snorkelers with marked trails and resting rafts.

Seven cannons, an 18th century anchor, and a large gun barrel are marked by buoys.

Scuba certification is not needed to view the underwater world through helmet diving. Photo: M. Strohofer.

SNORKEL BOAT TRIPS

An alternative to snorkeling from shore is to take a snorkel boat trip. Trips usually last three-and-a-half to four hours, and the snorkel boat operators provide all of the dive equipment and instruction. Snorkel boats operate from April to December depending on weather.

See Appendix 5 for listings of snorkeling yachts, cruises and operators.

HELMET DIVING

This is the perfect alternative to scuba diving and snorkeling for those interested in seeing the underwater world. There is no need to remove your glasses or contact lenses, no need to learn how to breathe through a snorkel, and

Lit from behind, the giant purple sea fan reveals its fused together, lace-like branches. Photo: J. Cancelmo.

you don't even have to know how to swim! Even young children can safely helmet dive. After a 15-minute briefing, you are ready to go.

The operation is simple. The divers descend down the ladder at the stern of the boat until they reach chest-deep water. Then the helmets are placed over their heads and they proceed to the bottom, which is between 10 and 15 feet (3-5 m) deep. Air is continually pumped to the diver from diaphragm compressors on the boat.

The divers are taken on a professionally supervised walk amid colorful coral reefs teeming with fish. Divers are encouraged to hand-feed friendly angelfish, hogfish, sergeant majors, coneys and, even on occasion, snappers. Underwater portraits are available upon request. Although the entire cruise takes about 3 hours, divers should expect to be underwater between 20 and 30 minutes. The helmet diving season runs from May through October.

See Appendix 6 for the listing of helmet diving operators.

CHAPTER **X**   MARINE LIFE

On a map, Bermuda appears to be totally isolated from the Caribbean, but Bermuda is actually connected to the Bahamas, Florida, and the Caribbean islands by the Gulf Stream. Warm nutrient-rich waters that constantly bathe the island bring along larvae and other surprises. In 1983, when the Caribbean was swept by a long-spined sea urchin plague, it was only weeks after the Florida urchins were impacted that the Bermuda urchin population was also affected. So it's no surprise that Bermuda's reefs and fish are very Caribbean-like. Because of the warmth of the Gulf Stream, Bermuda hosts the northernmost coral reefs in the Western Hemisphere. Stony or hard corals are very prolific and include several brain coral varieties: star, flower, rose and lettuce corals. There is an absence of elkhorn and staghorn coral in Bermuda. Soft corals include the knobby and spiny candelabrum, bushy soft corals, sea feathers, giant sea plumes and massive purple sea fans.

Bermuda's reefs host colorful sponge growth, but the formations are small and comparatively sparse. Pink-tipped sea anemones are common as are moon jellyfish, hydroids and fire coral. A sample of mollusks found include octopus, squid and sea hares. Lobsters, shrimps, arrow crabs, hermit crabs and other crustaceans can also be seen. Starfishes, brittle stars, sea urchins, and sea cucumbers represent the echinoderms in Bermuda.

The fish population of Bermuda, whose decline was of great concern a decade ago, has made a strong comeback. Common to reefs, but by no means a complete listing, are the blue and queen angelfishes, butterflyfishes, stoplight and midnight blue parrotfishes, colorful wrasses, goatfishes, squirrelfishes, snappers, chubs, grunts, damselfishes, jacks, triggerfishes, soapfishes, barracudas, bonefishes and tarpons. Sea turtles are increasingly seen. Stingrays, spotted eagle rays and sharks are rarely encountered. For the record, the island's endemic species include the Bermuda half-beak (*Hemiramphus bermudensis*), Verril's hermit crab (*Calcinus verrilli*), and the anemone shrimp (*Periclimenes anthophilus*). And the "stay-aways" in Bermuda include bristle worms, sea urchins, Portuguese man-o'war jellyfish, fire coral, and mantis shrimp known in Bermuda as a "split-thumb". Following is a sample of fishes and invertebrates common to Bermuda's reefs.

This wide-angle close-up photo dramatizes a purple-tipped sea anemone. This animal is often a shelter for tiny crustaceans and fish that hide behind its wavering tentacles. Photo: J. Cancelmo.

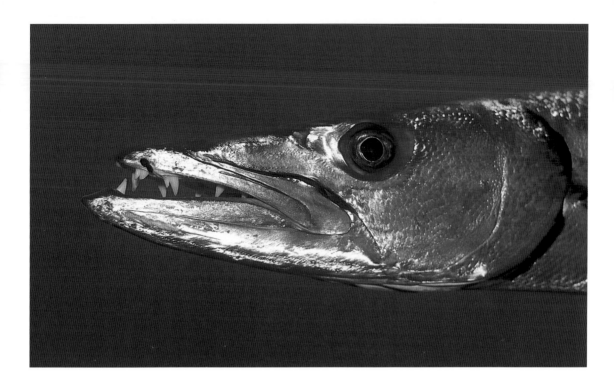

*Great Barracuda (*Sphyraena barracuda*) can reach lengths of over 5 feet (1.5 m). Usually camera-shy, they like to maintain a distance between themselves and divers. Photo: J. Cancelmo.*

FISHES

Barracuda

Built for speed with a silvery, streamlined body and equipped with an impressive set of dentures, there is no doubt that the great barracuda (*Sphyraena barracuda*) is an effective predator, getting much deserved respect on the reef. Curious like cats, cudas like to follow divers around the reef and sometimes even circle around. But when confronted, they normally back off. It's unusual to have a problem with a barracuda, but if you encounter one that does not back off, or darkens in coloration, it's wise to swim away. And never intentionally provoke a barracuda.

Blue Angelfish

Several species of angelfish are found in Bermuda, but the blue angelfish (*Holacanthus bermudensis*) holds an obvious special status. Known locally as the Bermuda angelfish, this disc-shaped reef resident is also common in Florida but is rarely seen in the Caribbean. The Bermuda angelfish is easily identified by the striking yellow borders on its tail and pectoral fins as well as its "spot free" nape (unlike the queen angelfish). The Bermuda angelfish is somewhat shy during the day, but like many fish, is more approachable at night.

Grouper

Grouper, members of the Serranidae family, are well represented in Bermuda with more than a dozen species. They are solitary and carnivorous, and most go through sex changes from female to male. Grouper have huge mouths and many have the ability to radically change their colors and markings. They also are known to spawn in mass. The most common grouper seen on Bermuda reefs is the coney (*Cephalopholis fulvas*). The red hind (*Epinephelus guttatus*), the graysby (*Cephalopholis cruentata*), the tiger grouper (*Myceteroperca tigris*), and the Nassau grouper (*Epinephelus striatus*) are all seen in Bermuda. Bermudians refer to the Nassau grouper as a "hamlet". The largest and most curious of the grouper family is the jewfish (*Epinephelus itajara*). These monsters reach hundreds of pounds in size but are rarely seen on the reef.

Longsnout Seahorse

Unlike most fish, the longsnout seahorse (*Hippocampus reidi*) as other seahorses, incubate eggs in the male's pouch. Talk about the perennial Mr. Mom! The seahorse is a member of the pipefish family, but it is so distinctive that there's no way to mistake its identity. The challenge is finding one. Longsnouts are typically 2 to 4 inches (5 to 10 cm) in length. They are often found in shallow waters near docks or on wreckage. The divemasters know where to find them. One special spot is the barges in Castle Harbour, just out from the Grotto Bay Resort.

*Blue angelfish (*Holacanthus bermudensis*) are known locally as the Bermuda angelfish. This reef resident is easily identified by the bright yellow border on its tail. Photo: J. Cancelmo.*

*Longsnout seahorses (*Hippocampus reidi*) are typically 2 to 4 inches (5 to 10 cm) in length so they can be difficult to find. Ask your divemaster where to find them. Photo: J. Cancelmo.*

Moray eels, like this green moray
(Gymnothorax funebris), often hide
in crevices and are harmless unless
provoked. Photo: M. Strohofer.

Moray Eels

Several species of eels are found in Bermuda. The most common is the spotted moray (*Gymnothorax moringa*). The large, green moray (*Gymnothorax funebris*) is perhaps the most intimidating but certainly no threat. They open and close their mouths constantly for respiration, not in readiness to attack. When unprovoked, morays are seldom aggressive. They usually back off if you get too close. Other morays less common in Bermuda are the goldentail moray (*Gymnothorax miliaris*) and the smaller chain moray (*Echidna catenata*).

*The puddingwife (*Halichoeres radiatus) *is one of the largest and most colorful of the wrasses. Photo: J. Cancelmo.*

*The often pugnacious sergeant major (*Abudefduf saxatilis) *knows no fear. Photo: J. Cancelmo.*

Puddingwife

Closely related to parrotfish, the wrasses are somewhat smaller and more elongated. And instead of the "parrot beaks", wrasses have distinctive sharp "buck teeth". Like parrotfish, wrasses go through phases and color changes. Unlike parrotfish, wrasses feed on shells and sea urchins. The numerous species of wrasses found in Bermuda range in size from 3 inches (8 cm) to 18 inches (46 cm) long. The largest and one of the most colorful of the wrasses is the puddingwife (*Halichoeres radiatus*). This blue-green colored wrasse often appears electric in daylight. To identify it, look for a dark dot at the base of its pectoral fin. Adults have five white blotches along its upper back.

Sergeant Major

It's been said that if sergeant majors (*Abudefduf saxatilis*) grew to be 6 feet long (2 m), it would not be safe to go in the ocean. Fortunately these feisty and often aggressive fish only reach 6 inches (15 cm) in length. In Bermuda, sergeant majors are also called cow pollys. Their golden and black chevron distinguishes them from the other damselfish varieties. If you encounter an unusually upset or hyper damselfish, it's likely that you are too close to its cluster of purple eggs or its private patch of algae. Be warned that these tiny dynamos are known to take a nip or two on exposed skin.

Snapper

Snapper get their name from the snapping action of their jaws when caught by fishermen. Grey snapper (*Lutjanus griseus*) are pale to dark grey and typically seen in schools. They have little fear of an approaching diver and to fishermen, they are the most cunning fish on the reef. The schoolmaster (*Lutjanus apodus*) is silver with distinctive yellow fins. Juvenile schoolmaster are often seen swimming solitary in schools of grey snapper. The yellowtail (*Ocyurus chrysurus*) have a bright yellow tail and a distinctive yellow stripe across their mid-body. They swim alone and in schools, and feed mainly on small fish and crustaceans.

Stoplight Parrotfish

One of the more amazing aspects of certain fish is the ability to change sex. The stoplight parrotfish (*Sparisoma viride*) is one of those "switchers" that can change color and change sex. If you see one that's mainly green with three diagonal bands on its head and with bright yellow areas at the base of its tail and near its trailing edge, it's in a "terminal male" color phase. The stoplight, also known as the green parrotfish, has powerful jaws that are used to scrape algae from the coral polyps. As these diligent vegetarians work the reef, they often excrete clouds of powdery residue.

*Prized as a game fish, tarpon (*Megalops atlanticus*) are primitive and powerful. Photo: J. Cancelmo.*

Tarpon

Tarpon (*Megalops atlanticus*) are the kings of sport fish. They grow up to 8 feet (2.5m) in length and look like giant, silvery herrings with upturned jaws. Tarpon have huge, shiny scales, and a single dorsal fin with a long, ribbon-like trailing fin. These extremely fast swimmers reach weights of more than 350 pounds (159 kg). They feed on small bait fish and are especially attracted to schooling silversides. Tarpon are often spotted at overhangs near the Western Blue Cut.

*Stoplight Parotfish (*Sparisoma viride*) are colorful and can be heard grinding the coral with their beak-like teeth. Photo: J. Cancelmo.*

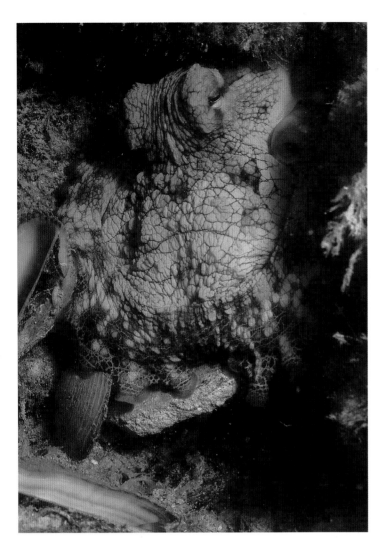

*The Atlantic octopus (*Octopus vulgaris*) normally hides during the day, but can often be found by the empty shells scattered near its lair. Photo: J. Cancelmo.*

INVERTEBRATES

Octopus

The octopus is a night hunter that feeds on crustaceans and bivalves. During the day it normally hides in crevices and holes in the reef. Look for the empty shells piled near its lair. Able to change colors in seconds, the octopus has a brain more greatly developed than any other invertebrate. The common Atlantic octopus (*Octopus vulgaris*) is globe-shaped with four pairs of thick arms. A tubular water siphon is under its neck and each of its arms has two rows of suction cups. The common octopus can be reddish-brown one minute and in the blink-of-an-eye later change to a near white or other color variation. When threatened, it ejects an ink cloud and darts for cover.

Pederson's Cleaner Shrimp

The Pederson's cleaner shrimp (*Periclimenes pedersoni*) is found among the tentacles of the purple-tipped sea anemone. This symbiotic relationship does nothing for the anemone but affords the shrimp protection from predators. The anemone shrimp (*Periclimenes anthophilus*) is another shrimp found in anemones and is one of Bermuda's few endemic animals. This delicate, nearly transparent shrimp has tiny pincers and long white tentacles. Other shrimp found in Bermuda include the banded coral shrimp (*Stenopus hispidud*), and the red hingeback (*Rhynchocinetes rugulosa*).

The Pederson's cleaner shrimp (Periclimenes pedersoni) is often seen ridding fish of parasites. Photo: J. Cancelmo.

Purple tunicates (Clavelina picta), also known as sea squirts, form gelatinous colonies and filter the surrounding water for nutrients. Photo: J. Cancelmo.

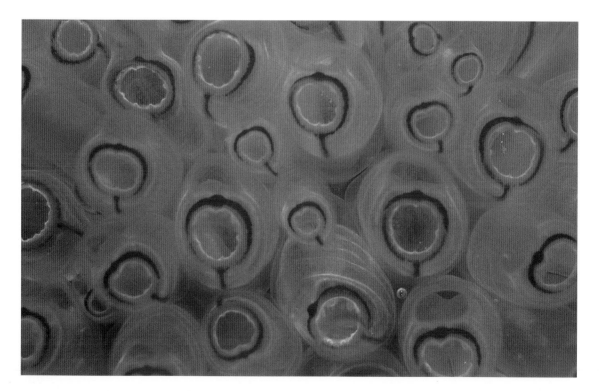

Purple Tunicate

The semi-translucent purple tunicate or sea squirt (*Clavelina picta*) attach themselves to rocks or cling to sea rods forming colonies that look like a cluster of jelly-like tubes. Sometimes bluish or even pinkish in hue, each tube is ringed in a darker shade near its opening. These gelatinous animals syphon particles of food from the water.

Sea Urchins

Sea urchins are echinoderms (same family as sea stars). The most common sea urchins found in Bermuda are the spiny sea urchins (*Diadema antillarum*), the pencil sea urchin (*Eucidaris tribuloides*) and the purple sea urchin (*Lytechinus variegates*). Divers need to be careful near the spiny urchins, especially when there's a surge. Their long, very sharp spines are brittle and can easily puncture a diver's skin and snap off, leaving a broken piece painfully embedded. Bermudians sometimes call urchins "sea eggs". Their mouth on the underside has five white teeth they use to graze on algae.

Spiny Lobster

In Bermuda, spiny lobsters (*Panulirus argus*) mate from mid to late spring and spawn in early summer. Millions of eggs are released, but the survival rate is low. When backed in a hole or crevice, their protruding and moving antennae often give them away. Big ones have body lengths of 24 inches (61 cm) or more. They are protected by law.

Avoid getting too close to sea urchins, especially if there is a current or surge. Their sharp spines can easily puncture the skin. Photo: J. Cancelmo.

*Look under ledges and in shadowy crevices to spot the prized spiny lobster (*Panulirus argus*). Photo: J. Cancelmo.*

APPENDIX 1

SAFETY AND EMERGENCY INFORMATION

All of the dive operators have the marine safety equipment required by the Bermuda Marine Board as well as first aid kits and oxygen. Boat captains, divemasters, guides and instructors are properly trained to respond to an emergency. Decompression problems are infrequent since most of the dive sites are shallow.

The ultimate responsibility for safety, however, rests with the diver. With new information becoming available regarding decompression sickness and multiple dives per day over a period of days, divers are urged to make conservative use of dive tables and dive computers.

Always pay strict attention to the divemaster's pre-dive briefing. Important information is conveyed that may include safety aspects for getting off and on the boat, a description of the dive site and marine life, and communication signals. Use the buddy system at all times and always ascend slowly—no more than 40 feet (12 m) per minute. For the last 30 feet (9 m) to the surface, an ascent rate of 20 feet (6 m) per minute is suggested.

Emergency Numbers

While these telephone numbers were correct at the time of publication, if diving outside the supervision of a dive operation, they should be verified upon arrival.

Recompresion Chamber   **236-2345**
King Edwards VII Memorial Hospital
Point Finger Road and Berry Hill Road,
Paget

Ambulance	**911**
Air and Sea Rescue	**297-1010**
Marine Police	**295-0011**
Divers Alert Network	**(919) 684-8111**
(emergency only)	**(919) 684-4326**
DAN Travel Assist Emergency	
	(800) DAN-EVAC

Divers Alert Network (DAN)

The Divers Alert Network (DAN), a non-profit membership organization associated with Duke University Medical Center, operates a 24-hour Diving Emergency Hotline number (919) 684-8111 (dive emergencies only) to provide divers and physicians with medical advice on treating diving injuries. DAN also operates a Dive Safety and Medical Information Line from 8:30 A.M. to 5 P.M. Eastern Time for non-emergency dive medical inquiries. DAN can also organize air evacuation to a recompression chamber as well as emergency medical evacuation for non-dive-related injuries for members. Since many emergency room physicians do not know how to properly treat diving injuries, it is highly recommended that in the event of an accident, you have the physician consult a DAN doctor specializing in diving medicine.

All DAN members receive $100,000 emergency medical evacuation assistance and a subscription to the dive safety magazine, Alert Diver. New members receive the DAN Dive and Travel Medical Guide and can buy up to $250,000 of dive accident insurance. DAN offers emergency oxygen first-aid training, and provides funding and consulting for recompression chambers worldwide. They also conduct diving research at Duke University Medical Center's Center for Hyperbaric Medicine and Environmental Physiology. DAN's address is The Peter B. Bennett Center, 6 West Colony Place, Durham, NC 27705. To join call (800) 446-2671 in the U.S. and Canada or (919) 684-2948. Web site: www.diversalertnetwork.org

APPENDIX 2

BERMUDA TOURISM OFFICES

For additional information contact one of the offices of the Bermuda Department of Tourism. A booklet containing travel tips and a map of the island are available free.

Website   www.bermudatourism.com

Atlanta

245 Peachtree Center Avenue NE, Suite 803
Atlanta, GA 30303
(404) 524-1541

New York

675 3rd Ave.
New York, NY 10017
(212) 818-9800
(800) 223-6106

United Kingdom

% Hills Bafour
Norcutt House
36 Southwark Bridge Road
London SE1 9EU
020-7202-6382

APPENDIX 3

BERMUDA'S FORTS AND NATURE TRAILS

Bermuda Forts

Since the early 1600s, Bermuda used its many coastal fortifications to protect against foreign invasion. Today, several are easily accessible to the public and offer glorious scenery and a fascinating look into the past.

Pembroke Parish
Fort Hamilton
Happy Valley Road
Towering over Hamilton Harbor with enormous 18-tone guns, this is where the Duke of Wellington met his match.

St. George's Parish
Fort St. Catherine
Coot Pond Road
Built in 1614, it was designed with a draw bridge over a dry moat.

Gates Fort
Cut Road
A tiny fort with a splendid view.

Sandys Parish
Royal Naval Dockyard
Ireland Island North
This 19th Century colossal fortification was used by Britain during the Revolutionary War.

Scaur Hill Fort Park
Elys Harbour
Originally built at a high elevation to procect against an invasion of the Dockyard, this fort played a role in WWII.

Nature Trails

Pembroke Parish
Admiralty House Park
Spanish Point
16 acres (6.5 ha) of walking trails, sea caves, enclosed coves and picnic areas

Bermuda Railway Trail
West End
21-mile-long (34 km) scenic east to west trail for walkers

Hamilton Parish
Blue Hole Park
12 acres (4.9 ha) with a nearby pond and caves

Devonshire Parish
Devonshire Marsh
Vesey Street
36 acres (14.6 ha) with an abundance of birds and wildlife

Sandys Parish
Heydon Trust
Elys Harbour
22 acres (8.9 ha) with trails, swimming, and view of Great Sound

Hog Bay Park
38 acres (15.4 ha) of trails and gardens with lush vegetation

St. George's Parish
Lovers Lane
Ferry Point Park
5 acres (2 ha) near a beach and old fort

Smith's Parish
Spittal Pond Nature Reserve
South Road
34 acres (13.8 ha) a favorite for bird watchers

APPENDIX 4

SCUBA DIVING OPERATORS

The scuba operators listed here all offer full certification as well as resort courses. Lesson schedules, boat destinations and departure times vary, so it is best to inquire first to find the desired diving for your level. In addition, only some of the shops offer night dives. All of the dive operators run at least two boat trips a day.

Visit the dive operators' websites for the most up-to-date information.

Blue Water Divers and Watersports, Ltd.
PO Box SN 165
Southampton SN BX
Tel: (441) 234-1034, (888) 434-8323
Fax: (441) 232-3670
URL: www.divebermuda.com
E-mail: somerset@cwbda.bm
1. Robinson's Marina, Somerset Bridge
   Tel: (441) 234-1034
2. Wyndham Resort and Spa
   Tel: (441) 234-4034
3. Elbow Beach Hotel
   Tel: (441) 232-2909

Dive Bermuda Ltd.
PO Box HM 237
Hamilton HM AX
Fax: (441) 234-5180
URL: www.bermudascuba.com
E-mail: info@bermudascuba.com
1. Hamilton Dive Center
   Fairmont Hamilton Princess Hotel
   Tel: (441) 295-9485
2. Southampton Dive Center
   Fairmont Southampton Hotel
   Tel: (441) 238-2332

Triangle Diving, Ltd.
Grotto Bay Beach Hotel
11 Blue Hole Hill
Bailey's Bay, CR 04
Tel: (441) 293-7319
URL: www.trianglediving.com
E-mail: deron@trianglediving.com

Appendix 5

Snorkeling Operators

Every major hotel on the water rents gear for snorkeling off the hotel beach. To reach reefs farther offshore, the boat operators listed below specialize in snorkel trips.

Bermuda Barefoot Cruises Ltd.
(441) 236-3498
E-mail: barefoot@ibl.bm
URL: www.bermudabarefootcruises.com
Departs from Hamilton Harbour

Bermuda Water Tours Ltd.
(441) 236-1500
Departs from Ferry Terminal, Hamilton

Sun Deck Cruises
(441) 293-2640
Departs from St. George's

Haywards Snorkeling & Glass Bottom Boat Cruises
(441) 236-9894
Departs from next to Ferry Terminal, Hamilton

Jessie James Cruises
(441) 296-5801
E-mail: jessiejames@northrock.bm
URL: www.jessiejames.bm
Departs from Albuoy's Point, Hamilton

Pitman's Snorkeling
(441) 234-0700
Departs from Somerset Bridge, Sandys

Salt Kettle Yacht Charters Ltd.
(441) 236-4863
Departs from Salt Kettle

Snorkel Look
(441) 293-7319
E-mail: scubaluk@ibl.bm
Departs from Grotto Bay Beach Hotel

Fantasea Bermuda
(441) 236-1300
E-mail: info@fantasea.bm
URL: www.fantasea.bm
Departs from Albuoy's Point, Royal Naval Dockyard; Waterlot Inn in Southampton

Hat Trick Charters
(441) 291-4978
Departs from Royal Naval Dockyard

Longtail Cruises
(441) 236-4482
E-mail: info@ibl.bm
Departs from Darrell's Wharf

Sail Bermuda Yacht Charters
(441) 236-9613
Departs from Albuoy's Point, Hamilton Princess, Darrell's Wharf

APPENDIX 6

HELMET DIVING OPERATORS

Bermuda Bell Diving
PO Box FL 281
Flatts FL BX
Tel: (441) 292-4434
Fax: (441) 295-7235
URL: www.belldive.bm
E-mail:belldive@ibl.bm
Flatts Village, Smith's, Royal Naval Dockyard

Greg Hartley's Under Sea Adventures, Ltd.
PO Box SB 194
Sandys SB BX
Tel: (441) 234-2861
Fax: (441) 234-3000
URL: www.hartleybermuda.com
E-mail: hartley@ibl.bm
Watford Bridge, Somerset

Peppercorn Diving Adventures
The Deliverance
Ordnance Island
St. Georges GE 05
Tel: (441) 297-1459
Fax: (441) 297-8460
E-mail: adventure@cwbda.com
Ordnance Island, St. George's

INDEX

A **boldface** page number denotes a picture caption.
An <u>underlined</u> page number indicates detailed treatment.